New Orde

JoyDivision

BEST WISHES

— Claude Flowers

Dreams Never End   *Claude Flowers*

Edited by Chris Charlesworth.
Cover & book designed by Michael Bell Design.
Picture research by Nikki Russell.

ISBN 0.7119.4308.7 Order No. OP 47742

Exclusive Distributors:
Book Sales Limited, 8/9 Frith Street, London W1V 5TZ, UK.
Music Sales Corporation, 257 Park Avenue South, New York, NY 10010, USA.
Music Sales Pty Limited, 120 Rothschild Avenue, Rosebery, NSW 2018, Australia.
To the Music Trade only:
Music Sales Limited, 8/9, Frith Street, London W1V 5TZ, UK.

Photo credits:
Peter Anderson / SIN: 4 / 5, 46, 53, 63TR, 81, 96T,101,116B, 121T; Bob Berg / Retna: 79B, 125R;
Bob Bromide: 54, 85, 107T; Andrew Catlin / SIN: 47, 99T, 100T&B; Kevin Cummins: front cover, 8,
10 / 11, 12, 14T&B, 15, 17, 20, 40/41, 60, 92, 103B, 104, 108, 113L, 120; Steve Double: back cover, 65,
90, 105, 113R, 121B, 123, 125L; Robert Ellis / The Rock Library: back cover; Greg Freeman / SIN: 97;
Jeff Hemmings / SIN: 102; Jayne Houghton / SIN: 118, 119; Tim Jarvis / Retna: 115L; Bob Leafe / Starfile:
51, 74R, 75; LFI: 48, 58L&R, 62, 63BL, 64, 68, 69, 70, 71, 72 / 73, 78T, 88 / 9, 94, 99B, 103T, 110, 124;
Leon Morris / Redferns: 55; Pictorial Press: 56; Barry Plummer: 36, 38; Chuck Pulin / Starfile: 45R, 82, 84;
Steve Rapport / Retna: 95; Rex Features: 77T&B, 78B, 79T, 93, 111, 113R, 115R, 117; Louise Rhodes /
SIN: 80; Zbysiu Rodak / SIN: 74L, 96B, 107B; Tom Sheehan: 6, 42, 45L, 57, 87BL, 112, 116T, 122;
Paul Slattery: 9, 18 / 19, 23, 24, 25, 27, 28, 29, 30, 31, 32, 33, 34, 35, 37, 39; Steve Speller / Retna:
66 / 67; Chris Taylor / Retna: 87; Ian Tilton / SIN: 86; Etienne Tourdour / Rock Photos: 49, 52;
Alison Turner / SIN: 44; Howard Tyler / Retna: 50; Stephen Wright: 59, 83, 98, 109;
Russell Young / Retna: 76;

New Order+ Joy Division

"The shadow of my sorrow. Let's see, 'tis very true.
My griefs lie all within and these external manners of
laments are mere shadows to the unseen grief which swells
with silence in the tortured soul.
There lies the substance." *Richard II, Act IV, Scene ii*

Introduction

I may have heard New Order on Long Island's new wave radio station WLIR *before* 1982 (we still called it "new wave" back then), but I didn't actually *know* it was New Order until I sat by the radio one autumn night, dying to find out who had performed this great song about, "Ooh, you've got blue eyes, ooh, you've got green eyes, ooh, you've got grey eyes." Jennifer Califano, the girl I'd had a massive crush on at the time, had just moved to Levittown with her mom, and this wonderful song expressed *just how I felt*. Unfortunately, the DJ hadn't announced the title of the cut, so I spent the next year or so hunting around for anything with the name New Order and stuff about "eyes" on it. First I ended up getting some bizarre 12" single designed to look like a floppy disc, then I heard this song called 'Age Of Consent' from the album *Power, Corruption And Lies*, which made me forget about the "eyes" thing for a little bit. I took all my record coupons down to the local Record World store and exchanged them for one of the prettiest looking LP's I had ever seen. I laid on my bed with the window cracked open, listening to music of a kind I hadn't heard anyone do before.

Then came an article in the original *Creem* magazine, from when *Creem* was funnier than shit and they'd get Sting or somebody to chew on a Boy Howdy can, and the article was all about New Order. They looked, in the picture at least, like an odd bunch of characters because they were all dressed informally and sitting on top of cases of beer, except for one dark-haired fellow who stood in front of the others and whom I presumed to be the lead singer. The name Joy Division cropped up. I heard 'Love Will Tear Us Apart' on the radio. Another record to hunt for.

I learned that the "eyes song" was called 'Temptation' and bought a New Order EP with 'Temptation' on it, but this was a different version from the one I liked. Found 'Love Will Tear Us Apart'. Found 'Temptation'. Bought a Joy Division tape called *Closer* and I *swear* that two songs into it, I thought I was gonna puke. Really. Something about it was just... off. I put that one away.

Low Life came out. *Brotherhood*. I saw New Order in concert for the first time and thought I'd seen God. Tried *Closer* again and this time I could take it. Other songs started sounding really good: 'Transmission', 'Novelty', 'Ceremony'. Began looking for more clippings, more records. Never had the dough to get the really valuable ones, but my stepfather's friend Jack Guy told me about this incredible Joy Division live album he'd seen in Bleeker Bob's with this sturdy, hard cover on it. Jack didn't know if it was a bootleg or not. I wanted to know more. Think about doing a fanzine, then decide on a book. Fit it in around work and college. Long-distance phone calls. Waking up at ten in the morning, going to bed at dawn the next day. Folks worried 'cause they say I'm listening to all this "I want to die" stuff. I play them 'Isolation'. Whew, hard to get happy after that one.

I think New Order, Joy Division, and their satellites Revenge, Electronic, and The Other Two have created some of the best music ever written. When they suck, they suck big time, and right now I think *Republic* is *really* sucky (in five years' time I might reconsider; I'll get back to you on that one), but when they hit the mark they make me glad and they make me cry and they make me excited. They make me grateful that I've spent over a decade of my life listening to their music. If I could go back in time to any period at all I'd go to May 17, 1980 and throw the fucker who would have killed John Lennon under a train, then I'd knock on Ian Curtis' front door, give him a big hug and tell him it's all alright. "Why don't you talk it out with Debbie and Hooky and Barney and Stephen and Rob and Tony and everyone else who loves you? You're okay. Don't be a doofus, man. We're gonna *need* you."

Then I'd make sure I got Jennifer Califano's address before she moved.

Opposite: clockwise, from top right: Bernard Sumner, Steve Morris, Gillian Gilbert and Peter Hook.

A lot of people have given me their time, knowledge, and support during the writing of this book. I'd like to take this opportunity to thank Peter Hook, Tony Wilson, Michael Shamberg, Rob Gretton, Tom Atencio, Brett Wickens, Doug Reyes, Kelly Behun, Sheryl Simmons, Tina Simmons, Mark Geiger and Mitch at Triad, Bill Bently, Peter Saville, Tim Haves, Jason Bruder, John Simons, Mike Powers, Rodney Ho, Chris Shea, Kathi Reilly, Rick Van Santvoord, Frank Garone, Joanne Altieri, Laurel Amtower, Chelle and Linda, Dave "You know me" Semingsen, Dave Burdick, Lance Goodwin, Kathy Monahan, Dave Sim, Gerhard and Los Bros for inspiration, James, Jet, Jasper and Elwood, Warren Kohler Sr. and Karen for keeping the manuscripts safe and loving music as much as I do, all the Fly people wide awake in America, Zooropa, Asia and the Underground, Chris Charlesworth and Andrew King at Omnibus, the Dixons, the Kohlers, the Blairs, the Yeatters, and most of all, Mom and Dad for their advice, their patience, and their faith. I love you both. Spring, this one's for you.

This is the way, step inside.

Claude Flowers, December 1994

Opposite: Bernard Sumner, nee Albrecht.
Above: Joy Division on the streets of Stockport, July 1979; Bernard, Ian Curtis, Peter Hook and Steve Morris.

Manchester

The ravaging by Hitler's bombers and post-war foreign competition sped Manchester's deterioration. Once the greatest city of the Industrial Revolution, by the 1950's many proud factories were simply shut down and abandoned. Slums were cleared, then swept away.

Bernard Dicken and Peter Hook were raised in this city. Childhood pranksters and close friends, they graduated together from school at age l6. Barney, with two 'O' levels to his credit, found a job at a cartoon studio. Hooky used his one 'O' level to get work at the Manchester docks. Four years passed, the two young men fell out of touch, and as their friends settled down, they had no reason to expect that their lives would be any different from their parents'.

All of that changed on July 20, 1976, when London's foremost punk rock band The Sex Pistols played the Manchester Free Trade Hall. Fresh from a residency at the capital's 100 Club, and known to Peter Hook through reams of press clippings, The Sex Pistols played a Manchester gig which lured Hook from home, and inspired him to invite Bernard Dicken and mutual friend Terry Mason along for the night. They witnessed a performance of strong bravado and swagger, short on actual talent, and yet they were absolutely captivated by how much fun The Sex Pistols were having, despite their technical inadequacies. Hook, Mason, and Dicken resolved to form a band of their own, simply to liven up their spare time. Dicken laughed, "If they can do it, we can!" The next morning, he bought himself a guitar.

Dicken's shiny new Gibson SG guitar, little amplifier, and instruction book took his mind away from the drudgery of his day job. Since Dicken had beaten him to his first choice of a six-string, Peter Hook purchased an electric bass, and Terry Mason managed to finance a drumkit. They found rehearsal space above the local Black Swan Pub, but still needed a name and a singer for their band. The name came fairly easily: they called themselves The Stiff Kittens, a title given to them either by local rock heroes The Buzzcocks, or coined by a neighbour whose cat had a miscarriage.

Finding a singer was a little harder. The Stiff Kittens taped a note at the local record store requesting a vocalist, and several Mancunians responded, many of them excited about punk music after catching The Sex Pistols at the Free Trade Hall, or on the TV programme *So It Goes*, hosted by ITV anchorman Tony Wilson. Everyone, it seemed, suddenly wanted to be in a band. Half a dozen applicants were turned down, but a seventh, Ian Curtis of Macclesfield, was accepted without an audition. The Stiff Kittens knew him as a friendly concertgoer, and they'd met him at several gigs. He was in.

Ian knew a lot more about rock and roll than his bandmates. His fiancée, Debbie Woodruffe, had turned him on to Iggy Pop's music in 1975, and he started bringing his favourite albums by Iggy and The Doors to band rehearsals. He worked days in a factory, but his heart was with poetry and literature, and he spent his spare time reading books by J. G. Ballard, William S. Burroughs, T. S. Eliot, and German and Russian philosophers. These writers had inspired him to try his hand at poems, and as the lead singer of The Stiff Kittens, he'd rearrange stanzas to fit the band's music. Early attempts produced cocky, blustery songs like 'Gutz', 'Tension', 'The Kill', 'At A Later Date' and 'You're No Good For Me', as well as improvised cover versions of 'Louie Louie'. The tracks had little personality, they were unfocused and frantic, but they allowed the group to escape to a world of their own.

By the spring of l977, The Stiff Kittens felt confident enough to play before an audience, and promoter Richard Boon booked them as support for The Buzzcocks' gig of May 29 at Manchester's Electric Circus club.

New Order + Joy Division

Previous page:
Warsaw, on stage at Rafters,
Manchester, June 1977.
Opposite: Steve Brotherdale.

The Electric Circus was the hippest venue in town, and The Buzzcocks were revered by local fans, so this was quite a début for the quartet. They all must have been incredibly nervous as the date of the show loomed closer.

On the day before the concert, Terry Mason apparently suffered a crisis of faith in his abilities as a drummer, and decided he wasn't good enough to play in public. He became the band's manager, and his first assignment was to find a replacement drummer before Sunday's concert! He discovered a Didsbury resident named Tony Tabac, and within a few hours, taught him the drum parts of The Stiff Kittens' repertoire. It was a crash course for Tabac, but he was prepared by showtime to join Dicken, Curtis and Hook onstage at the Electric Circus. The Stiff Kittens had arrived – sort of.

Peter Hook, Bernard Dicken, Ian Curtis and Tony Tabac did indeed perform as support for The Buzzcocks, but not as The Stiff Kittens. Either because they had grown to dislike the tag, or because they felt a new line-up called for a new moniker, the quartet entered the Electric Circus calling themselves Warsaw. Supposedly, the name originated from David Bowie's 'Warszawa' but the album *Low* that featured the song hadn't even been released yet, so this story is probably untrue. More likely it was an expression of the group's love for European fashions and imagery, which was reflected in their clothing: button-up shirts, ties, slacks, an armband for Barney Dicken (which immediately instigated rumours that he was a Nazi) and a jaunty leather cap for Hook. Cosmopolitan as they looked, they were unable to hide their stage fright, ripping through their set as fast as possible and not speaking between songs. Ian shouted in a heavy, working class accent, which made his lyrics incomprehensible. Most of the crowd was unmoved by this performance, but music critic Paul Morley became their first fan, admiring their, "Twinkling evil charm." Warsaw returned to their rehearsal room and began booking more gigs.

Now that they had some idea of what to expect from playing in front of a crowd, the band grew in confidence. Warsaw's second performance was rather theatrical, thanks to Ian Curtis and his love of the ever-volatile Iggy Pop. Scheduled to open for punk rockers Fast Breeder at the Manchester bar Rafters, Warsaw were shocked when the headliners decided to go on first, and were furious when Fast Breeder didn't finish their set until after midnight. Warsaw took the stage before a near-empty club at 1:30 in the morning, just as their equipment began to malfunction. This sent Ian into a frenzy. He dived to the floor, shattered bottles, and threatened to slice up the remaining clientèle. Promoter and Rafters disc jockey Robert Gretton knew every group in the region, but this one fascinated him. "Warsaw was just different," he recalled. "I thought they were the best band I'd ever seen." He would not forget them.

All of the band members continued performing at night for fun more than for profit. Tony Tabac left in June due to personality conflicts, replaced by an acquaintance named Steve Brotherdale. The arrival of some new blood fired the musicians' imaginations, and Warsaw's début rehearsal with Brotherdale yielded the band's first masterpiece. Unlike the macho fantasies that comprised Warsaw's song catalogue to this point, the track 'Novelty' was a mature observation about the advantages and disadvantages of playing music. The refrain "What you gonna do when the novelty is gone" was directed by Ian not only to his audience and his bandmates, but to himself as well. Warsaw were challenging the beliefs of themselves and people around them. Warsaw had found a cause.

The quartet met several times over the next month for a series of intensive rehearsals. These culminated in a July 18, 1977 trip to Pennine Sound Studios where they recorded a demo tape which they hoped would attract media attention, get them booked at bigger clubs, and be a document of what the group had accomplished at that period of their lives. Unable to afford much studio time, they had to record all songs in one take. The sessions, which included 'Inside The Line', 'Gutz', 'At A Later Date', 'The Kill' and 'You're No Good For Me' (but strangely, not 'Novelty') lasted from early afternoon until one in the morning. Each band member proudly clutched his own copy of the tape when Warsaw walked out into the night air. With luck, it would lead to better things.

Newlywed Steve Brotherdale certainly had both eyes open for opportunities, and since he could not make a living off the meagre earnings he was getting from Warsaw concerts, he found extra work as a session musician for rising stars The Panik. The Panik were recording a single entitled 'It Won't Sell', and although the title later proved sadly prophetic, they seemed to have a lot going for them at the time, especially in having Rob Gretton as their manager. Brotherdale defected to The Panik because he thought they would become more successful than Warsaw, and during a party that summer, he tried to get Ian Curtis to jump camps as well. Ian attempted to sing along to a copy of 'It Won't Sell' but his voice was incompatible with the music. Thanking Steve for the offer, Ian shrugged, "Well, I might as well go back to Warsaw."

Warsaw again posted notices for a drummer, and 19-year-old Stephen Morris of Ian's home town Macclesfield called to schedule an audition. Morris had played clarinet at Kings School, but like most people of his age, turned his attention to rock instruments with the advent of punk. He'd formed a group of his own, got a job at his father's kitchen fitting business when that group broke up, and had hoped to play music again ever since. Barney reportedly needled the younger man for enjoying ballroom dancing, but Stephen responded with a dry sense of humour which Warsaw liked. Equally important, he was a great drummer. Stephen Morris was voted into the group.

Manchester's arts community suffered a major blow that Autumn. In October of 1977, the Electric Circus, the club where Warsaw and many other local groups had got their start, was forced to close its doors forever for breaking city fire regulations. The owners scheduled two nights of "farewell" concerts to pay homage to the venue, with Warsaw as part of the October 1 lineup, alongside The Panik and several others. The invitation to be part of the Electric Circus' last weekend was terribly exciting to the band, and they felt delighted to receive it.

Imagine, then, their utter disappointment when October 1 came and the promoters told Warsaw that there was no room on the schedule for them to play. Ian wept, but recovered after he was told Warsaw could play the final night, October 2. Barney confused much of the audience when he took the stage and just prior to playing 'At A Later Date,' shouted, "You all forgot Rudolf Hess!" Actually, the Nazi war criminal was on many people's minds, having just suffered cardiac arrest in Spandau Prison. This bizarre lament for someone Barney viewed only as a sickly old man fuelled rumours that he was a Nazi sympathiser. His inarticulate outburst would follow him and his bandmates around for years to come.

The crowd's surprise at Barney Dicken's comment matched Warsaw's shock when a representative from Virgin Records appeared at their dressing room door with a document for them to sign. Unknown to Warsaw, both shows were being taped for release as a live album, and Warsaw needed to give legal permission for Virgin to include a song of theirs on the LP. Warsaw signed, and the rep. scurried away.

Many influential people attended the Electric Circus show. The closing of interested in the future of the Manchester music scene was on hand to assess and promote the neighbourhood's rising stars. Warsaw were often

picked out as being one of Manchester's brightest hopes. Paul Morley gave the quartet another favourable write-up in *NME*, and a journalist from *New Music News* had decent things to say about them as well. Another spectator was ITV television celebrity Tony Wilson, guitarist in The Negatives, a band scheduled for the October 1 show. "I came on the wrong night," Wilson said. "I brought my guitar, but it was the wrong night. This was the first time that many of us felt within ourselves that Warsaw was the major group. I'd seen them a couple of times before that, but that was the central night for me, and a lot of people."

Nevertheless, Warsaw were having trouble getting booked for concerts because the demo tape they were sending to booking agents was three months out of date and no longer accurately represented the band. To many club owners, the Warsaw they heard on tape sounded just like every other punk rock band in town, and were therefore not worth caring about. Without the Electric Circus around, good concert venues were at a premium, and competition to play anywhere was probably intense. Warsaw fell by the wayside. Fall and winter passed quietly for the group, with just a handful of public performances. Having nobody to play for but themselves, their friendship and their delight over simply creating music kept them together, whereas a band seeking fame and fortune might have cracked. Warsaw learned to articulate their ideas, and evolved into a tight, self-styled unit. Hooky liked to play bass like a guitar rather than as a rhythm instrument, and he and Barney discovered mutual gifts for melody that they would bounce around, one instrument mimicking the other. Stephen dreamed up eccentric time signatures to play on his drums. Ian's lyrics became increasingly introspective and he abandoned his harsh screams for a deep, resonant baritone. Even if the world seemed against them, the band thought, "We'll show them," and forged onwards. Nothing could stop Warsaw. Nothing.

T. J. Davidson, the owner of a local recording studio, admired the re-vamped Warsaw. In December of '77, he offered to produce, engineer, manufacture and distribute an EP of the band's music. They accepted, and recorded four songs that would comprise *An Ideal For Living.* The opening track, 'Warsaw', began with a joltingly loud *a cappella* verse, but was otherwise unremarkable. 'No Love Lost' told the tale of a female prisoner of war held captive in a Nazi brothel, and was inspired by a book Ian had read entitled *The House of Dolls* (the title even cropped up in one of the lyrics). Six seconds into the song, Ian could be heard breathing in the left-hand speaker. In order to get a crisp sound on T. J. Davidson's four-track recorder, many of the instruments and vocal tracks were recorded in just one speaker or the other. This technique, known as "hard panning", had been around since the late 1960's. Unfortunately, it dated the songs, making them sound very primitive. The recording did not do the songs justice.

The mid-tempo 'Leaders Of Men' and hyperactive 'Failures (Of The Modern Man)', both scathing pieces of social criticism, dismissed history as – to quote The Sex Pistols – a "mad parade" of cruelties. The lyrics branded humanity as weak and evil. Ian Curtis adopted this cynical point of view for most of his songs to come. The tracks tested the limits of his vocal range, but his visions knew no bounds.

Five thousand copies of *An Ideal For Living* were pressed as 7" singles, and the quality of the vinyl that the factory used to make them turned out to be awful. Warsaw were so embarrassed by the sound of the records that the band refused to let them be released. Davidson complied, and put the discs into storage.

Joy Division

The House of Dolls continued to haunt Ian Curtis, especially the image of innocent human beings enslaved for the entertainment of others. In some respects, it seemed to be the perfect metaphor for the way Warsaw had been manipulated by the music industry around them. They felt like prostitutes at times, forced to stay in a small wing of a very large prison (obscurity) until called upon by the wardens (music industry power brokers). The name for the prostitutes' prison wing in *The House of Dolls,* and the name Warsaw assumed at the start of 1978, was Joy Division.

The "Joy" of the title contrasted humorously with the band's pessimistic outlook. The new name also ended a problem clubs were having in mistaking Warsaw for Warsaw Pakt, a punk group which had just released an album. Joy Division made their public début on January 25, 1978.

The show took place at Pip's in Manchester, advertised as a Warsaw concert to help fans make the transition from one name to the other. Despite some confusion that almost caused Ian to miss the gig entirely (he'd had a few too many drinks before showtime), and a fight in the audience, which muscled dockworker Peter Hook broke up, the concert announced Joy Division as the quartet's official new name. They resolved to change it again if anyone left the group, or died.

Stiff and Chiswick Records hosted a battle of the bands at Rafters on April 14, 1978. Joy Division and sixteen other acts showed up for the competition, the winners getting a recording contract with the eclectic Stiff label, and, presumably, fame and fortune. The playing order was determined at random, because everyone wanted to perform first before the judges lost interest and went home. The last name drawn from the hat read, "Joy Division".

Waiting for their turn, the group walked to the bar for a drink, and sat next to ITV's Tony Wilson. One of the music industry power brokers who held the key to success, Wilson had distinguished himself as the first English TV host to feature punk rock. No doubt on hand this evening to do some talent scouting himself, he arrived with Warsaw's Electric Circus performance strong in his mind. Certainly, one of the bandmembers should introduce themselves? Ian introduced himself by grabbing Wilson on the collar and saying, "You bastard! You put Buzzcocks and Sex Pistols and all those others on the telly, what about us?" Barney and Steve prised their singer off and dragged him away. Hooky, meanwhile, tried to con everyone he saw into taking the "headlining" spot, but nobody fell for his scheme. Joy Division were stuck at last place.

They walked onstage at around ten minutes to two in the morning, and blazed through four songs that none of the judges and few of the audience had stayed to hear. They felt miserable, believing they had missed an important opportunity. Yet all was not lost: Rob Gretton complimented them on a "brilliant" set, as did a friend of theirs, a college student named Gillian Gilbert. Even Tony Wilson enjoyed them. The contest had been a real "Stiff Test", but Joy Division were winning over all the right people in spite of themselves.

A few days later, Ian shared wonderful news with his bandmates. After visiting the offices of RCA Records, hoping to get some free Iggy Pop posters, he met Derek Branwood, the company's Northwest promotions manager. Ian gave Branwood a copy of *An Ideal For Living*, and Branwood liked it enough to pass it on to his assistant Richard Searling and Grapevine Records president John Anderson, who were forming their own punk record label. Searling and Anderson wanted to release a full-length Joy Division LP, and the band thought this a great idea. They even attempted to fulfil the duo's request for a cover version of the song 'Keep On Keeping On', but the best they could do was adapt some of the licks

Ian, Hulme, Manchester, January 1979.

into a new composition they entitled 'Interzone', named after a William S. Burroughs novel.

Joy Division had already perfected their material onstage, so recording the songs was a quick and easy process lasting only the first four days in May. They taped eleven songs, with Arrow Studios engineer Robert Auger operating the recording equipment. 'The Drawback' began the album on a powerful note, full of galloping drum tracks, catchy melodies, and Ian's vocals mixed loudly enough so that his lyrics could be understood. All four songs from *An Ideal For Living* were re-recorded. The entire band sang the chorus of 'Walked In Line', a bold anti-Nazi statement that could only discourage the festering suspicions about Joy Division's political sympathies. The wonderful 'Novelty' was also taped, the slow and lumbering intro suddenly charging into the body of the song.

'Transmission', written in protest at the decline of pirate radio stations, featured an instantly memorable chorus – "Dance, dance, dance, dance, dance to the radio" – which would make it an audience favourite at Joy Division concerts. 'Ice Age' followed, a vivid fantasy about an Earth of the future locked in an eternal winter, and 'Shadowplay' ended the album on a malevolent note, the final thundering chord and cymbal crash drifting off into nothingness. Here, at last, was a disc that gave indications of the scope of Joy Division's potential.

The bandmembers signed contracts with Searling and Anderson on the night of May 4, right after they had finished recording, only to find out that they'd agreed to a royalty deal far below the British average. Anderson overdubbed synthesizers onto 'No Love Lost' and 'Transmission' to give the LP a richer sound, and this distressed Joy Division even further. The band loved music first and foremost, and to have an outsider tamper with their songs worried them. They allowed Searling to present Anderson's final mix to RCA, but made no promises about letting anybody release it.

As Stephen, Ian and Hooky tried to forget their troubles by rehearsing at T. J. Davidson's, Rafters DJ Rob Gretton appeared in the doorway. They knew he was a fan, but had no idea why he'd shown up. "What's he doing here?" they wondered. Barney arrived shortly thereafter, and with a grin he explained, "This is our new manager."

Terry Mason was a very dear friend to everyone in Joy Division, but he just wasn't a very good manager. Gretton, on the other hand, was experienced and genuinely excited about the band. Having left The Panik because they wouldn't listen to him, Gretton wanted to manage Joy Division, and all four bandmembers agreed he was the man to do it. "I used to be sort of a roadie for Joy Division as well," Gretton later said. Terry Mason became the group's road manager, and Gretton told everyone to sit tight and see how the "RCA Album" resolved itself.

Virgin Records released the compilation LP *Short Circuit: Live at the Electric Circus* in June. As the first publicly available release to feature Joy Division, it exposed many people to the group, although unfortunately, Virgin had chosen the mediocre 'At A Later Date' – with Barney's quote about Rudolf Hess – to represent them. *Short Circuit* didn't serve the band well.

About a week after the record's release, Joy Division appeared at the Factory, a weekly event held at Manchester's West Indian Russel Club. The Factory was co-organised by Tony Wilson and an actor named Alan Erasmus in an attempt to revitalise the Manchester scene, which still hadn't recovered from the loss of the Electric Circus. As Wilson explained, the Factory club, "Came about purely because Alan Erasmus and I started managing The Durutti Column, which wasn't so much a band that existed, but one we created around two members of another group. We rehearsed them for three months, and by that time, you want to do your first gig.

We decided we didn't like any of the places in Manchester, Rafters had become boring, there was no interesting place. So we decided that the best thing to do was actually open a place, which is what we did. We went into the projects of Manchester, which is the equivalent of, say, Bedford Stuyvesant town in New York. We went to this guy who was a white gangster, trying to borrow the Russel Club just so The Durutti Column could play there. We thought, 'If we're borrowing it for one night, which the guy said we could do, why don't we borrow it for four consecutive Friday nights, give the event a name, give it an identity, invite some of the other groups we know onto the bill.' And that's how it grew. By the time that May came, there were four nights and a whole load of bands played. We approached Joy Division to play in June, and they said, 'Yeah'."

The name Factory came about not as a tribute to Andy Warhol's Factory Club in New York, as many have believed, but, "by accident, really." Wilson said, "I was walking down the street in Manchester. Alan Erasmus saw a sign that read, 'Factory Warehouse Sale,' and said, 'Why don't we call (the new club) Factory?' At the time I said, 'That's fine,' but the Warhol connection never occurred to me."

Joy Division's Factory Night was advertised with a slick-looking poster designed by an art student named Peter Saville. Wilson recalled meeting Saville after a Patti Smith concert: "I was walking out, and this kid came up and said, 'Uh, hey, I know you do a lot of things, if you ever need a designer, I'm the man, I'm the greatest. I'm a young kid, but I'm a great designer.' I got his phone number, and two or three months later I rang him up and said, 'Do a poster (for Factory).' That was the beginning of my relationship with Peter Saville.

"I asked a close friend about him, a friend of his, who said, 'Oh, no, not Saville, he's late with everything!' The one job (Saville had) done while at the Polytechnic, the art school, was a brochure for Amek mixing desks.

Mayflower Ballroom, Manchester,
July 1979.

He'd done one of those, and his friend, whose company it was, said, 'He did one, but he didn't do the next one even though it was so good because he doesn't get it fucking together. It was so late!'" Wilson was willing to overlook Saville's tendency to take a long time on projects if it meant having the best designer in town working for the Factory. Like Joy Division, Tony Wilson cared more about art than money or business. It was his first love, and he was unwilling to compromise his tastes even if it meant not always making the most profitable business decisions. He wanted Saville, and the association proved mutually beneficial for years to come: Saville found a steady source of work, and Factory, unlike the punk institutions of the day, attained an elegant, modern image that set it apart from all others.

After letting *An Ideal For Living* gather dust for six months, Joy Division responded to public demand for a record and released the disc through its own Enigma label. Steve typed a letter to distributors promoting the, "special folding sleeve which turns into a 14"x14" full-colour/black-white poster – a real treat for all 'Collector's Item' fans." Barney designed the sleeve under his new stage name, Bernard Albrecht, Albrecht being the name of a company he liked. This package was a real muckraker, Barney intentionally annoying the band's critics. The cover shot pictured a Hitler Youth, "Joy Division" was written in flowing Germanic script, an excerpt from 'Leaders Of Men' captioned a photo of a Polish child captured by a stormtrooper intended to warn against misplaced trust in politicians, and the performance credits featured umlauts over every vowel. The inside portion of the sleeve revealed the band's true feelings about governments; a portrait of them in a jail cell, captives at the hands of another power.

One bit of text read, "This is not a concept EP. It is an enigma." The double entendre rang true, only not everyone understood that the pseudo-fascist themes of the cover were intended as an anti-fascist statement. Happily, most fans understood Joy Division's confrontational brand of social criticism, and they snapped up all of the five thousand copies available. This was very impressive for a band not known out of their immediate area. The 7" was never reprinted, and Steve Morris' prediction came true: *An Ideal For Living* became a wildly popular collector's item, doubling and redoubling in price on the used record market as the rest of the nation discovered the group.

By summer's end, RCA made an offer regarding Joy Division's album. They'd press it, see how well it sold, and if it did well, finance a second LP, but the band would receive no cash advance, and royalties would be minimal. Rob Gretton retaliated with the band's terms: ten thousand pounds up front, and a royalty of fifteen percent on every record sold. John Anderson replied in plain terms: "Fuck off."

A solicitor representing Joy Division studied the recording contract, then warned Anderson that the band had signed a document of questionable legality, and that he and Searling would be taken to court if they tried to release the album or hold the band to the agreement. Joy Division offered to buy the master tapes to cut the producers' expenses, which they accepted, and the quartet borrowed money from their parents to raise the amount they needed. They paid for the tapes, and both parties went their separate ways.

Infrequent gigging occupied Joy Division into the fall, but steady practising outside the public eye honed their talents even more. By the time they played the Factory club again on October 20, the press was really taking notice of them. To accommodate reporters, Joy Division issued a re-packaged 12" version of *An Ideal For Living*, with improved sound quality and less offensive artwork (an office tower covered by scaffolding, indicative of the EP being improved). Journalists and fans acquired all twelve hundred copies, and Joy Division once again found itself without a record to represent them.

In August '78, Roger Eagle and Pete Fulwell, managers of the popular Liverpool club Eric's, called Tony Wilson with a proposal to start Eric's Records, a label spotlighting unsigned talent. Eagle and Fulwell told Wilson, "We've only brought out one record, that was a year ago. We're going to restart (the record label), and we want you to be our talent scout." "Great," Wilson replied, always ready to promote the Manchester scene. "Fucking great! What a wonderful idea!" He made an appointment to see them, and drove South to Liverpool.

During his ride, Wilson envisioned the first release on Eric's Records as a sampler featuring Joy Division, The Durutti Column, and two other bands. When he arrived, the trio discussed the idea.

"Let's do a 12" single," Fulwell said, "Joy Division and Durutti Column having one track each on side one, and some other groups can have one track each on side two."

"No," Wilson said, "I've got this idea. I saw a copy of Santana's *Abraxas* LP at a friend's house. It was an import from Thailand, and the sleeve was printed on tissue paper and sealed in plastic. Really weird. We shouldn't be doing a 12" EP, we should be doing two 7" EPs with four groups having two tracks each. It'll be the first double 7" since The Beatles' *Magical Mystery Tour.* Plus, we should do it with this tissue paper sealed in plastic."

Eagle and Fulwell disagreed with Wilson, and although they parted as friends, their business association had come to an end. On his way home to Manchester, Tony Wilson thought, "What about me?" He talked about his plan of releasing a two-disc set with Alan Erasmus: "Let's do it ourselves. I had the idea when I was there, they didn't want to do it, let's do it ourselves." Erasmus liked the idea. Naming their label after their nightclub, they called their record company Factory.

In October 1978, just as the last copies of the *An Ideal For Living* 12" were disappearing from the shelves, Tony Wilson spent three thousand pounds of the money he'd inherited from his mother to subsidise *A Factory Sample,* a double 7" EP featuring tracks from John Dowie, Cabaret Voltaire, The Durutti Column, and Joy Division. Joy Division's songs, 'Digital' and 'Glass', were recorded on October 11 at Cargo Studios with producer Martin Hannett mixing the sound. Hannett's previous credits included records by The Buzzcocks and John Cooper-Clarke, and he'd also helped distribute the 12" *An Ideal For Living* to record stores. His idea of what Joy Division should sound like was a lot subtler but no less intense than the heavy metal thunder that made up much of the band's live show. He used studio effects to give the tracks depth, and although the band were never entirely happy with anyone's interpretation of the Joy Division sound besides their own, they couldn't deny that Hannett added new levels of emotion to their songs. Hannett, like Wilson, Erasmus, Saville and Gretton, would become one of Joy Division's staunchest supporters and closest confidants.

'Digital', a meditation on paranoia and insanity, centred around a horrified chant of, "Day in! Day out!," Ian Curtis sounding berserk. The frantic music intensified the feeling of disarray. 'Glass' was a straight-ahead rocker, which Hannett embellished with ambient noises mixed just below the instruments. In this producer's hands, Joy Division's tales of moral, social, and mental decay found the perfect accomplice. It was a match made in Hell. No other group could come close to sculpting nightmares so detailed or believable. With Martin Hannett focusing their message, Joy Division became the voice of everyone's fears and doubts.

Electric Ballroom, London, October 1979.

Tony Wilson scheduled *A Factory Sample* for release in 1978, but Peter Saville missed the deadline for completing the artwork, and the release date was pushed back to January 1979. Wilson, however, felt determined to give copies of the EP as Christmas presents to all the musicians who'd played on it, so on Christmas Eve he photocopied Saville's cover designs and made his own sleeves with paper and glue, sliding the already-pressed discs in and delivering them himself to the homes of twenty musicians, including Ian Curtis, Stephen Morris, Bernard Albrecht and Peter Hook. Factory Records' origins were quaintly low-key and personable.

Joy Division made their London début at the Hope and Anchor in Islington on December 27, 1978. Despite the cheap admission price of sixty pence per ticket, only twenty or thirty people attended, many of them journalists. They witnessed a powerful show that proved Joy Division were ready for success. The music was tight and strong, the vocals articulate and believable. Equally important, Joy Division were becoming mesmerising entertainers. Barney stood still out of necessity: he couldn't move and play guitar or his new toy of choice, the synthesizer, at the same time. But Steve Morris flailed with energy, battering his drumset in many

Ian at Central Sound Studios, Manchester, January 1979.

directions at once, and Peter Hook hunched over with his knees bent and back arched forward, playing with his bass swinging below his knees, visibly having a wonderful time. Ian Curtis especially attracted attention. He danced onstage, shaking his body, spinning his arms, and singing with a look of hypnotised awe on his sweat-drenched face. The only drawback to his dancing was his tendency to move too far away from the microphone while singing – the mic couldn't pick up his voice.

One of Ian's dance moves resembled a *grand mal* epileptic seizure, which suited one of Joy Division's new songs perfectly. 'She's Lost Control' told the story of an epileptic woman so humiliated by her condition that she goes to the top of a skyscraper and commits suicide by having a seizure

Mayflower, July 1979.

which forces her to fall from a window, her last words being, "I've lost control again." 'She's Lost Control' was based on fact – the lyrics read like a primer on epilepsy – and incredibly catchy. What the fans who sang and danced to 'She's Lost Control' did not know was that Ian Curtis had written the song from personal experience: he was epileptic, and took medication to keep his condition in check. Strobe lights and physical or mental stress were apparently among the triggers that could set off an attack for him, and Joy Division repeatedly had to tell club owners to use only steady spotlights at their concerts. For Ian's sake, flashing lights were strictly prohibited.

A little over a month later, on January 31, 1979, Joy Division returned to London, this time to record some material for Radio One disc jockey John Peel. Peel, an avid supporter of new groups, often invited his favourite acts to record four songs in a high-tech BBC studio, and would then air the Peel sessions on the radio for all to hear. Joy Division's session consisted of two new songs, 'Exercise One', and Barney's synthesizer workout 'Insight', plus two fan favourites, 'She's Lost Control' and 'Transmission'. Free of the "RCA Album's" interfering keyboards, 'Transmission' came alive, the song gradually building in tension and complexity, until Ian Curtis screamed, "We can dance," and all the energy shot outwards, dissipating with Stephen Morris' drumbeat which slowed down and finally stopped, as if a record player had been unplugged in the middle of the song. The Peel Session was first broadcast on St Valentine's Day, giving the band the national airplay they so desperately needed to become anything more than a regional success.

Around this time, Joy Division came to the attention of Martin Rushent, a producer who owned Genetic Records, a subsidiary of Radar Records, itself a subsidiary of the corporate giant Warner Brothers. Rushent wanted to work with Joy Division, and if he and the band got along, there was every reason to believe they would be signed to Genetic, and essentially, Warner Brothers. A deal like this could lead to international distribution of Joy Division records, promotion, radio airplay, world tours, everything a band dreams about. Joy Division recorded a demotape under Rushent's supervision, which turned out to everyone's liking, and the producer looked into making a deal with Warner Brothers. This seemed like the perfect opportunity: a chance for Joy Division to make albums to the band's standards – without outside tampering – and release them internationally. Credibility and attention could both be theirs.

Joy Division said farewell to London with a show at the Moonlight Club, promoted by two music fans who called themselves Final Solution, after a Pere Ubu single, not after Adolf Hitler's plan for racial purity (this was another Nazi-related name that would get Joy Division in trouble). A good relationship formed, and whenever the band wanted to play in the capital, Rob Gretton knew he could count on Final Solution to make all the necessary arrangements.

The Genetic /Radar/Warner Brothers deal was on everybody's minds, including Tony Wilson's. He fully expected to lose them from Factory. He said, "Joy Division began to be very hot, and very famous people were talking about them after the *A Factory Sample* single. It was beginning to happen, they were beginning to get inquiries, and I was going out to London to meet with Martin Rushent... It was moving along quite seriously, and I wasn't concerned, it seemed like, 'this is what we do now.' Factory had just put out a record by Orchestral Manoeuvres in the Dark specifically to get them a deal, and we were in negotiations with Phonogram, various people.

"In 1976, the early days of punk, and throughout '77, there was very much a, 'fuck the major labels' attitude. 'Fuck the majors, we're the new

world.' But by the time '78 came along, there was a general acceptance that (small record companies) being a nursery for the majors was okay, it was cool, that's what you're meant to do.

"And suddenly, Rob Gretton turns to me one night and says, 'Hm. Tell you what, obviously we'll go to Warner Brothers and Radar soon, and sign up, but before going, why don't we do the first album here (on Factory), with you?' I said, 'That's an idea. Are you sure?' I thought it was kind of funny... I figured Rob was doing it as an experiment, but he was doing it to see if it would work. And if it would work, it would leave him free of getting fucked over by a big record company. Which indeed it did.

"So that was how the mood was changed. And of course, Joy Division later became successful. It then set the reverse mode, which is you don't want to sell to the majors."

With Martin Hannett producing, it took Joy Division less than a week to record a whole LP for Factory. Like all Factory projects, no contracts were involved, and the band were guaranteed fifty percent of all profits.

'Disorder' began the album on an energetic note. Martin Hannett's studio wizardry, Barney Albrecht's eerie synthesizers, and Ian Curtis' confused, frightened voice lent an emotional depth to what might have otherwise been an ordinary mid-tempo rock song, and the refrain, "I've got the spirit, but lose the feeling," captured the restless energy and thoughts of every young adult with no sense of purpose or direction. Immediately, 'Disorder' established that this would be a work which people could turn to as an expression of their own disenchantment. 'Day Of The Lords' dragged the listener in deeper, Ian repeatedly asking, "Where will it end?" as Stephen Morris' drums suggested heavy, zombie-like footsteps. The imaginary speech of a disillusioned politician to his selfish constituents in 'Candidate' echoed 'Leaders Of Men', showing that the band's faith in humanity had not been restored. Joy Division viciously attacked evil on every level.

Martin Hannett added the sound of an antique elevator to the beginning of 'Insight'. The door clanged shut, the "lift" ascended, and then the door opened and dispensed its passenger, Ian Curtis. He sounded dangerous here, warning, "I'm not afraid anymore!" to anyone who'd listen. Were these the fictional ramblings of a madman, or was Curtis expressing a pent-up aggression? Apparently his bandmates never thought to ask.

The monumental 'New Dawn Fades' revealed Joy Division in full bloom. With Hannett controlling the mixing board, the group were recorded at the height of their abilities and ambitions. The most telling line, the one which summed up the quartet's *modus operandi* and served as an omen for what would come of their explorations, was, "We'll give you everything and more, the strain's too much, can't take much more." Sadly, in rummaging through their Pandora's Box, they let hope get away. By not finding anything redeeming about life, Joy Division seemed worryingly closeminded. For those listeners who ignored lyrics, the music rocked, especially in concert, where 'New Dawn Fades' was thunderous.

Hannett channelled Ian Curtis' voice through numerous effects for the album's version of 'She's Lost Control', all of which distracted from the plot of the song and sounded cheesy after one listen. The spartan, almost clinical version they had recorded for John Peel did the song much more justice. Peter Hook's bassline and Steve Morris' shimmering cymbal crashes set a mood in 'Shadowplay' without the use of echo chambers or backwards tape loops, and the sound was enough to get Ian and Joy Division's growing legion of fans, "grooving to the silence without motion." The music of 'Wilderness' also invited dancing, while the lyrics catalogued examples of torture throughout the ages. They implied that "civilisation" was the real wilderness.

Mayflower, July 1979.

'Interzone' had undergone many changes since its recording for the "RCA Album". The basic track and lyric remained the same, but Joy Division layered a second lead vocal on top of the first, creating a dialogue between both voices. This altered the whole tempo of the song, giving it a momentum which the original lacked.

Bravely, perhaps stubbornly, Joy Division ended the record on a brooding, uncertain note, reiterating that their songs couldn't – or wouldn't – offer answers, only questions. 'I Remember Nothing' was a dirge haunted by mechanical droning noises and the crash of pipes and bottles in a lonely, empty room. Once again, Ian Curtis' voice was recorded twice, allowing him to interpret his words in two different ways. One voice would sing as the other spoke or shouted, then they would switch back and forth. A cleansing wind swept the music and voices away, but one last clang of metal and an explosion of broken glass threatened that a potential for violence remained. The album, painful and beautiful, smart and provocative, was a hell of a début.

Joy Division celebrated its completion by headlining a fund-raiser for the civil rights organisation Amnesty International. The May 3 gig at Eric's in Liverpool commanded a sparkling review from the *NME*'s Ian Wood, who closed by naming Joy Division, "An Important Band". But also an unlucky one, as the trouble-ridden "Factory Tour" of that month reaffirmed. The first night went well, but the promotional buttons Rob Gretton ordered for the Acklam Hall gig were misspelled, and fewer paying customers arrived than people on the guest list. Tony Wilson felt happy just to have a "Factory Night" in London, but it wasn't a proud moment for anyone else. OMD cancelled from the third and final show because they thought the stage was too small, and Ian Curtis lost his cool when the lights went out and he couldn't see to play guitar. He just stood there in the darkness, embarrassed and upset. For him, the evening had been ruined.

Joy Division's début album, *Unknown Pleasures*, came out during June, 1979. Tony Wilson spent ten thousand pounds of his own life savings to record and press the LP, much more than he'd expected to pay. Peter Saville and the band collaborated on the classy packaging, which, like the Factory club posters, set it apart from its contemporaries. Inspired by the line "Exploded star between us" in William S. Burroughs' *Who Is The Third That Walks Beside You?*, Barney found on page 111 of *The Cambridge Encyclopedia of Astronomy* a graph of the radio waves emitted by the first pulsar ever discovered. Saville used a reverse image of the graph – white on black, instead of black on white – on the front cover. On the back, he put the album title, band and company names, and catalogue number. Lacking a photo of Joy Division, or even the song titles, *Unknown Pleasures* looked stark and mysterious. The song credits appeared on the inner sleeve, as did a black and white photo from Ralph Gibson's book *The Somnambulist* of 'The Enchanted Hand', beckoning listeners towards the wonders and horrors inside, especially 'Disorder', which began, "I've been waiting for a guide to come and take me by the hand." This was one of many obscure jokes to come, contradicting the band's grim-faced image.

The extensive use of synthesizers on *Unknown Pleasures* surprised some listeners, despite the band's growing fascination with keyboards. Lately, Joy Division had walked onstage to the tune of Kraftwerk's electronic 'Trans-Europe Express', and Barney had dabbled with two synthesizers he'd built from kits, an ARP Omni II and a Powertran Transcendant 2000. He and Martin Hannett played synths on the LP along with the other instruments as an integral part of the songs as a whole, not to "fill-in" as John Anderson had done on the "RCA Album". Joy Division expressed concern that Hannett might be softening the power they had onstage, but fans could tell that the relationship only intensified the group's

potency. *Unknown Pleasures* sold briskly. Tony Wilson earned back his investment, and the band received three dollars for every album sold. They could afford to stay with Factory rather than risk dealing with a huge corporation or a major label. Rob Gretton's gamble had paid off. They could remain independent.

The only bad aspect of staying with Factory was that the company didn't have enough money to press as many records at any given time as the public demanded. Each lot of ten thousand albums had to completely sell out before Factory could finance another pressing of *Unknown Pleasures*. With only ten thousand copies available at any given time, the public was unable to buy enough copies within a week to make *Unknown Pleasures* a hit on the record charts. In addition, Tony Wilson admitted, "It was just going out to independent record stores. I used to deal with twenty-four different accounts. In those days, you went and acted as virtually your own distributor... At that level of work, you'll never get a chart position."

The critics fell in love with *Unknown Pleasures,* and wanted to speak with Joy Division to learn more about the individuals who had created such an incredible piece of work out of what seemed like thin air. The band ignored most interview requests. They insisted that people should decide for themselves what the songs meant, rather than seek out the group for the "real meanings". As another reason, they knew very well that journalists – who had mostly ignored them to this point – could promote a band as the "next big thing", then destroy them for "going commercial" right when they achieved success. Joy Division argued that self-promotion detracted from their songs, and found question and answer sessions boring and unenlightening. They especially grew tired of having to explain that they were not, and had never been, Nazi sympathisers! The reporters interpreted Joy Division's wariness as arrogance, and some articles collapsed into personal attacks against the band. Joy Division responded by cutting off contact with everyone but the underground press and fanzines.

June slipped by, with Joy Division broadening their public image by appearing on radio and television. They recorded 'Candidate', 'These Days', 'Atrocity Exhibition' (named after a book by J.G. Ballard) and 'Chance', later retitled 'Atmosphere', for Piccadilly Radio in Manchester, and performed a live rendition of 'She's Lost Control' during an episode of Granada TV's *What's On*. In July, they recorded definitive versions of 'Transmission' and 'Novelty' with Martin Hannett producing, as well as the brooding 'Dead Souls' (named after a novel by Gogol) and 'Something Must Break'. Two of the tracks, they decided, should come out as a single, and the others could be used when they needed them. August began well enough, Joy Division playing at a festival promoted and organised by Final Solution, but on the 13th, the whole band came very close to death...

Joy Division travelled five hundred gruelling miles that summer day to play London's Nashville Club, and when showtime arrived, they decided to open with 'Exercise One', a tune they'd not performed in concert for months. Their rustiness with the song, as well as their exhaustion from the trip, affected their performance. The club had been overbooked, and some fans had to pack into rooms adjacent to the auditorium itself, content with just listening to the band. To cap it all off, a shutterbug in the front row kept blinding everyone with his flashcubes, so Peter Hook, nerves and patience worn thin, stopped the guy by kicking his camera into pieces.

Joy Division's problems didn't end there! As Hook drove the band home that night, he noticed a lorry coming from an on-ramp and barrelling towards them. Before anything could be done, the vehicle smashed into Joy Division's van, tearing the back off and spilling musical equipment into both lanes of the road. "It appears that the lorry driver fell asleep," Rob Gretton told reporters.

During the end of summer, the band took part in the Leigh Valley Pop and Futurama Sci-Fi festivals, two high-profile gigs that allowed the group to play before large crowds. They also became involved in a quadruple-feature of films sponsored by Factory Records, named simply after its Factory catalogue number "Fac 9", and held at London's Scala Cinema. The film *Joy Division* by director Malcolm Whitehead, who would later become the man in charge of Factory's IKON video wing, was a seventeen-minute long document of the band rehearsing at T.J. Davidson's, as well as three songs from their Bowden Vale Youth Club concert. *No City Fun*, a twelve-minute short by Charles Salem, employed two cuts from *Unknown Pleasures* as its soundtrack. Both films were shot in 8 mm.

Only John Peel had given the band anything approaching broadcasting support, so Joy Division appeared on BBC 2's *Something Else* and Radio One's *Rock On* programmes to improve their profile a little more. A couple of days later, The Buzzcocks offered Joy Division the support slot on an

Electric Ballroom, October 1979.

upcoming UK tour. This certainly would draw attention to the band! On the down side of things, it would be an extensive undertaking, forcing Joy Division to travel long distances right after eight hours at work. On the up side, it would mean playing to lots of new people, who may not have heard Joy Division before, but might very well become fans. They accepted the offer.

Joy Division warmed up for the tour with two gigs in the Northwest, one a benefit for the Nashville Club, recently firebombed by neo-Nazis, and the other at the resurrected Factory. The latter was disrupted by a heckler, who Peter Hook put into his place by chasing him through the club. It was a bad omen for the tour, which would be marred by violence, bad acoustics, health problems for Ian, and the constant struggle to impress an audience who had come to see The Buzzcocks, and not necessarily Joy Division.

At other times, the cross-country jaunt saw Joy Division in top form, earning people's attentions and affections, and even being called back for encores. During a break in the tour, the band drove to Brussels, Belgium to play at the opening night party of a sugar refinery-cum-dance club Plan K. Headlining the show was William S. Burroughs, the writer who'd been such an inspiration to Ian Curtis. The delighted singer tried to introduce himself to his idol, but Burroughs wanted no part of him, and in a few cruel words, told him so. Ian was heartbroken, and walked away, in silence.

Amateurs filmed Joy Division's Plan K gig, as well as those of October 27 and 28 at the Manchester Apollo with The Buzzcocks. Besides the band's rare TV appearances, and the Malcolm Whitehead documentary, these would be among the few times Joy Division were captured on film. The scarcity of available footage of the band increased the group's aura of mystery, and would prove a real disappointment for future generations of fans who never got to see Joy Division in person.

Factory released the Joy Division single 'Transmission' b/w 'Novelty' near the end of The Buzzcocks tour. The scream at the end of 'Transmission', already chilling on the Peel Session version, was recorded several times with all the screams laid on top of one another for this rendition, and the effect was overwhelming. Tony Wilson thought the "Dance to the radio" chorus would prove irresistible to radio programmers, and considered hiring an outside source to plug the record to the stations. He alluded to this in Factory's *Newsletter And Shareholder Analysis* of that autumn: "Negotiations are under way even now with the big stall owners." But for whatever reason, Factory never hired a promotions representative, and the BBC ignored this cult favourite because it was, "Too gothic". As a result, 'Transmission' never sold as many copies as it deserved. In this light, the song's lamentation about the demise of pirate radio stations became especially quaint and ironic. 'Novelty' had undergone several changes since its first recording in 1978, and this take was more succinct and moving than any performance that had come before. Peter Saville chose the photos for the cover, using *Unknown Pleasures* as the inspiration for the photo of the nova on the front, and a high-speed snapshot of a BB passing through an electrical current – a "novelty" – on the back.

Another record came out in October with two Joy Division tracks on it, the Fast! Records compilation *Earcom 2: Contradiction*. 'Autosuggestion' was the closest Joy Division would ever come to expressing hope; its chorus, "Take a chance and say you tried," was equal parts subliminal message and positive reinforcement. 'From Safety To Where' stared into the future and asked, "Should we move on, or stay safely away?" This was Joy Division's present mindframe: should they continue to explore the dark side of life, or look to other subjects for inspiration? They chose the darkness. Their single-mindedness would limit the range of experience they could express in their music, but no other band travelled where they were going. No other band dared to. Their songs investigated madness.

The Buzzcocks tour ended with a two-night stand at London's Rainbow Theatre. When the final curtain had been lowered, promoter and Buzzcocks manager Richard Boon told Rob Gretton that his band had enjoyed touring with Joy Division, and wanted to continue the double-bill with a tour of North America. The concept of "carrying the best of Manchester to the States" sounded like the perfect idea, but there was one detail that couldn't be resolved: The Buzzcocks wanted to fly from venue to venue, and Joy Division could only afford to travel by coach. The two groups said goodbye, but Ian, a notorious prankster, couldn't let his fellow Mancunians go home without a little gift. As The Buzzcocks rode home that night, they noticed dozens of white mice dashing around inside their tour bus.

Joy Division had written two new songs during the past month. 'Love Will Tear Us Apart' was an instant smash, although some listeners pointed out that Barney's keyboard melodies recalled 'Then He Kissed Me' by the American girl group The Crystals. The chorus, unlike most Joy Division songs, mentioned the title of the song, and the arrangement, the hooks, everything about it made 'Love Will Tear Us Apart' the perfect pop song – except the lyrics, which described at length the disintegration of a marriage.

'24 Hours' was heartbreaking, a relentless procession of crushed, "hopes and past desires." The narrator sounded on the verge of hurting himself or someone else. "Gotta find my destiny," he warned, "before it gets too late." The music came in waves, each mightier than the last, ending on an uncertain note, nothing resolved, nothing gained. Ian Curtis wasn't telling if this song expressed how he really felt inside or if it was just a story, but in either case it stunned the listener into submission. '24 Hours' was their most troubling composition to date, but also one of their best. The paradox of Joy Division was that their songs got better as their moods got worse.

On the 26th of November, Joy Division recorded 'Love Will Tear Us Apart' and '24 Hours' as half of their second Peel Session. The other tracks they taped were the rollicking 'Sound Of Music,' a double bass guitar assault by Barney and Hooky which bore no resemblance to the Julie Andrews classic whatsoever, and 'Colony', a return to the social criticism so pervasive on *An Ideal For Living.* Tony Wilson of the BBC (a different Tony Wilson from the Factory chief) produced the session, first broadcast on the 10th of December and reproduced on bootlegs shortly thereafter. Demand for a new Joy Division record was high.

Ringing in 1980 with a private party in Manchester's Piccadilly Garden, Joy Division embarked on a European tour, beginning at the Paradiso Club in Amsterdam on Friday, January 11. The opening act never arrived, so Joy Division performed two sets, seventeen songs in all. The tour then cut through Holland and Belgium, where a shortage of hotel rooms forced Joy Division to sleep in a whorehouse – after "business hours", of course. West Germany treated the group better; they played at the Basement in Cologne, a gorgeous venue in a church cellar with an arched ceiling and adoring fans. The tour ended somewhat appropriately, considering the band's fascination with German culture, at Berlin's Kant Kino club. They returned home to Manchester on January 23, and took a few days off as a holiday.

It may have been on this European tour that Ian Curtis first met a woman from Holland with whom he fell in love. His marriage to Debbie apparently did not suffer as a result of it, and for a time, he managed to keep both relationships separate. But he would not be able to keep his mistress a secret from Debbie for long, and within four months, his infidelity would backfire on him, with dire consequences.

New Order + Joy Division

Joy Division became increasingly ambitious in the studio, and during March they recorded a huge number of songs with Martin Hannett: 'These Days', 'The Sound Of Music', 'Komakino', the rock and disco instrumentals 'Incubation' and 'As You Said', and the nine songs that would comprise their second album. They even attempted 'Love Will Tear Us Apart', but were unable to reproduce the music they heard in their heads onto studio tape. Tony Wilson lent Ian a copy of Frank Sinatra's *20 Greatest Hits* LP for inspiration, but nothing helped.

All four bandmembers dabbled with new instruments, Ian and Stephen trying their hand at keyboards, and Hooky teaching himself guitar. They slept during the day, having quit their jobs to play music full time, and spent dusk 'till dawn recording. This work schedule didn't improve Ian's health, and his epilepsy began to interrupt the recording sessions. It made him irritable, and on a few occasions, he suffered blackouts, one of which sent him crashing headfirst into a sink, which knocked him unconscious. The rest of the band found him lying on the floor.

Ian acted as *The Divine Comedy's* Virgil for the album's introductory 'Atrocity Exhibition', telling the listener, "This is the way, step inside." He introduced a carnival freak, a gladiator, murderers and even "The ones who try hard to succeed" as doomed losers, although a verse used in concert about strippers did not make it onto this recording. Where he had said, "I've been waiting for a guide to come and take me by the hand" at the start of the first album, here he *was* the guide: "Take my hand and I'll show you what was, it will be." Experience had shown him the truth, and the truth was ugly.

The music of 'Atrocity Exhibition' and indeed of much of this album was disturbing. Instruments were played slightly out of time with one another, paganistic drums tumbled until they nearly put listeners in a trance, and guitars grinded and howled without rhythm or rhyme. For the uninitiated, this noise could be physically unsettling, causing headaches, nausea, and certainly paranoia. The band's creation defied the rules of popular music. For Joy Division to have recorded 'Love Will Tear Us Apart' at the same period as 'Atrocity Exhibition' proved them to be either breathtakingly flexible or patently schizophrenic.

'Isolation' slipped deeper into the abyss. Stephen Morris' mechanical drumbeats and Barney Albrecht's keyboards, just slightly out of sync with the other instruments, confused and disconcerted. The lyrics were Curtis' most devastating, the real wallop coming shortly after the first chorus: "Mother, I'm trying, believe me, I'm doing the best that I can. I'm ashamed of the things I've been put through, I'm ashamed of the person I am. Isolation. Isolation. Isolation." A brief synthesizer reprise of 'Isolation' cleared one's head in time for 'Passover', where stress forced Ian to sing, "This is the crisis I knew had to come, destroying the balance I'd kept." The future seemed to hold no promise.

Hook and Albrecht played the undulating melody of 'Colony' in unison, while Stephen Morris' electronic drums tapped out beats in time with them both. The lyrics described a complete lack of trust in relationships; familial, social, religious, sexual, or otherwise. The protagonists left everything they had known to start a new life, but the "colonies" they established did not bring them happiness or peace. Problems could not be escaped, but neither, apparently, could they be resolved.

Peter Hook's bass dominated 'A Means To An End', and although Hook usually shared the lead vocals of this song with Ian Curtis when Joy Division performed it on stage, Ian sang this version alone. "I put my trust in you," he lamented, as Albrecht's guitar added a supplementary melody, plus yelps and echoes of Hook's basslines. Morris' drums – a sort of heartbeat – slowed down at the end and the song "died." Side one of the LP closed on a dark note, and side two would not offer comfort either.

Opposite: Electric Ballroom, October 1979.

'Heart And Soul' responded to arguments about all people being inherently decent by stating, "beyond all this good is the terror," every saint a powderkeg waiting to explode. Joy Division's powderkeg exploded on 'Twenty Four Hours', the band's most aggressive, articulate, and powerful composition. Every verse ended with a crushing statement of woe, including, "Look beyond the day in hand: there's nothing there at all", and, "Just for one moment I thought I'd got my way. Destiny unfolded, I watched it slip away." The search for truth had divested Ian of his illusions, and he confessed, "I never realised the lengths I'd have to go, all the darkest corners of a sense I didn't know." Naturally sensitive, by displaying his innermost thoughts he had destroyed his ego. He didn't know where he was going. The funereal 'The Eternal' showed him one possibility: inevitable death. 'Decades' showed him a fate far worse.

In 'Decades', Albrecht played a repeating synthesizer melody as Curtis sang of a Joy Division reunion ten or twenty years into the future. Watching home movies of the band in concert, the band-members would recall only, "the traumas and degenerations, the sorrows we suffered and never were freed." The thrill of making music would have long since died, and Joy Division would enter the ranks of the has-beens. People would ask, "Where have they been?" That Ian Curtis couldn't recognise Joy Division's greatness and contributions to rock and roll may have been the saddest tragedy of all.

At the end of 1979, Joy Division had received a letter from Jean-Pierre Turmel of the Sordide Sentimental record label, who requested two songs for a project creating *Gesamtkunstwerk*: "total art." Joy Division were intrigued, and sent him the beautiful, gentle 'Atmosphere' and 'Dead Souls' to work with. Turmel put the tracks on a limited edition 7" disc inside a full-colour folder and entitled the package *Licht Und Blindheit*, German for *Light and Blindness*. On one side of the folder was a Jean-François Jamoul painting of a cowled monk standing before a mountain range, on the other, Turmel's essay comparing stage performers to cave explorers, because they lose their sense of perspective when under the glare of spotlights. Rob Gretton's reaction? "I thought the wording was a bit over the top, but it was quite a nice package." *Licht Und Blindheit* was also frustratingly obscure, because only 1,578 copies were released. Fans who couldn't find a copy felt cheated, especially when by the band's own admission, 'Atmosphere' was one of the best things they'd ever recorded. It, too, was reproduced on bootlegs to meet popular demand.

During April 1980, Factory booked three nights of entertainment at London's Moonlight Club, and Joy Division appeared at all three shows unannounced. At the first concert, they encored with a cover of The Velvet Underground's 'Sister Ray', a brilliant ending to what had started as a sloppy gig. "You should hear our version of 'Louie Louie,'" Ian chuckled. The second evening went just as well, but on the third, Joy Division chose to also open for The Stranglers at the Rainbow Theatre, commuting to the Moonlight Club in time to headline. This was too trying for Ian Curtis. The lighting people at the Rainbow hadn't known of his epilepsy, and kept using strobes throughout Joy Division's performance. Despite his repeated requests to not use anything but steady spotlights, they wouldn't stop. At the end of the show, the flashing lights and heat overcame him, triggering a seizure which sent him sailing back into Steve Morris' drumkit. The audience interpreted this as a stunt Joy Division had planned for its "big finish", and applauded as Ian was carried to his dressing room. Five songs into the Moonlight gig, Ian had to be helped offstage again. Peter Hook took over on lead vocals, but the concert ended up being cut short anyway because it was late and the bar had to close. Regardless, the shows pointed out a depressing fact of life that the band would have to deal with: Ian's health was getting worse, and Joy Division's music was becoming too difficult for him to perform for extended periods of time. They would eventually have to change their sound, break up the group, or find a new singer.

Despite these problems, Joy Division booked their own US tour, to start on May 19 in New York City. Along the way they'd record a new single, the passionate, guitar-based 'Ceremony', and a dirge entitled 'Little Boy', after the atomic bomb, later re-named 'In A Lonely Place' in honour of the Humphrey Bogart film. They also scheduled a meeting with representatives of Warner Brothers Records, who not only were offering the band the creative autonomy they enjoyed on Factory, but a cool one million dollars, enough for them to record any sort of album they wanted. The major labels were coming around to the band's point of view. Nothing could stop Joy Division. Nothing.

The group booked warm-up gigs to practise for the tour, but Ian once again fell ill, and several of the concerts disintegrated into impromptu jam sessions, or were cancelled altogether. Fans actually rioted in protest, throwing bottles at Rob Gretton when he announced the band would not be coming back for an encore at one gig. For Rob's sake, or perhaps out of a perverse sense of humour, they encored with 'Atrocity Exhibition'.

Joy Division issued a three-track flexi-disc through Factory Records in

April. Intended as a gift to their supporters, it was literally free for the asking at stores that carried the band's releases. The freebie coupled 'Komakino' with 'Incubation' and 'As You Said', and there were plans to reprint the disc in lots of 25,000 until all fans owned one, the costs being covered by profits from Joy Division's upcoming single, 'Love Will Tear Us Apart.' Unfortunately, no more flexi-discs surfaced. Those that were available became high-priced collector's items, like most other Joy Division releases. "We said we'd (re-press the flexi) whenever they'd run out," Tony Wilson said, "just give them away in shops and stuff. (That Factory didn't) is a real failure on our part. We should do another (pressing) and just fuck everybody up." The reprints never came.

On April 28, 1980, Joy Division were filmed at T. J. Davidson's rehearsal studios performing 'Love Will Tear Us Apart'. The entire band knew the song would be a hit, and they agreed to make a video to promote it. Joy Division refused to mime or lip-sync, so they played the song live and had the best footage cued in time with the studio version. The end product was straightforward; it focused on the musicians' hands and faces, some red tinting was added, and an 'Enchanted Hand' led the viewer through the film. Eagle-eyed viewers noticed Ian Curtis' name scrawled among the graffiti on the door that opened and closed the video.

The final Joy Division concert planned before the group was to leave for America took place at Birmingham University's High Hall. 'Ceremony' and 'Decades' premièred that night, and this would be the first – and last – time Joy Division would ever perform these songs. When the show ended, the bandmembers had fulfilled the last of their English obligations. The artwork for *Closer* and 'Love Will Tear Us Apart' were ready, the records scheduled for release, and America lay before them. Joy Division never arrived.

New Order

As his recent lyrics had reflected, Ian Curtis was uncomfortable with being a celebrity. He wanted to reach many people with his music, but was confused and disturbed by the demands of fame. Although he was dedicating his life to a career most people could only dream of having, being a singer didn't make him any happier as a person. In a moment of rare confidence, he told Barney, "I feel like I'm caught in a whirlpool and I'm being dragged down and there's nothing I can do about it." Barney asked him to explain what he meant. He wouldn't.

According to one source close to the band who requested anonymity, Ian Curtis turned to the three women in his life for strength: his wife Debbie, his daughter Natalie, and his mistress. When Debbie discovered his infidelity, she asked Ian for a divorce. He was now afraid to leave his family for his girlfriend, and heartbroken at the thought of abandoning his Dutch lover. Ian felt that no matter what he did, he would end up hurting somebody he loved. He decided that he should leave; that if he was out of everyone's life, they'd be better off.

So on May 18, 1980, the eve of Joy Division's first American tour, he hanged himself.

Debbie found Ian's body that morning. The band were notified, the tour cancelled, and slowly, word leaked to the outside world. John Peel broke the news to many during his radio show, saying, "Bad news, lads. Ian Curtis of Joy Division has died." He broadcast 'Atmosphere' as a tribute. The press followed with numerous eulogies, some journalists romanticising and twisting the facts out of proportion, giving rise to a death cult which celebrated Ian's death as an artistic statement. Groups like Ultravox and Bauhaus emulated Joy Division's sense of dislocation, but failed to convey the band's tireless quest for truth. "Gloom and doom" became marketable traits from which musicians could earn money.

Ian Curtis had been more than just a singer to the surviving members of Joy Division. He had also been their friend, and they loved him dearly. Albrecht, Morris and Hook held a brief, uneasy band meeting to decide their future, and all agreed to stand by the group's original promise to retire the Joy Division name should the lineup ever change. They also decided never again to play any Joy Division songs, except the unrecorded 'Ceremony' and 'In A Lonely Place'. Insofar as they could, they wanted to start over with a clean slate. Ian's suicide caused them all to grow up very quickly. Their innocence died with him.

Factory released 'Love Will Tear Us Apart' backed with 'These Days' and an alternate take of 'Love Will Tear Us Apart' in June. The 12" single came in an elegant black and white sleeve featuring a statue of a weeping woman, while the 7" came in a fake "metal" cover, reminiscent of *Machine Head* by Deep Purple, or, as some people misinterpreted it, a tombstone. Both covers drew nasty criticism from people who thought Factory was exploiting Ian's death for profit, despite the fact Peter Saville had designed both months earlier. Even without the events of May 18, 1980, 'Love Will Tear Us Apart' had been a guaranteed hit, and with the sudden media attention resulting from Ian's death, or in spite of it, the disc went Top Ten in the British record charts. Joy Division, at last, had become superstars.

"I'm proud of Joy Division," Rob Gretton reminisced. "Joy Division were a very rocky (i.e. powerful) rock band. They were absolutely brilliant, and I'm proud of the whole thing they achieved, but I'm a bit disappointed that we didn't achieve what we could have. And obviously, I'm sad about what happened to Ian."

Closer, the last true Joy Division LP, hit the stores in July, and as some critics pointed out, its intense explorations of abject misery read like a suicide note. The album was greeted as a masterpiece, but the praise rang hollow for the remaining trio, because to them, *Closer* had been just

Clockwise from top right: Barney, Steve, Gillian and Hooky.

another step on the path they had chosen; they never intended it to be their last release. As the rest of the world studied this magnificent swan-song, Hook, Albrecht and Morris decided to start all over again, and drove to Western Works Studios in Sheffield to record a demo tape.

Stephen Morris handled most of the vocal chores on a session composed of 'Ceremony', 'Homage', 'Truth', and 'Dreams Never End'. For all practical purposes, the trio still was Joy Division, and its sound remained steeped in the melancholia which that band created. A few days later, they played backup on two songs with Kevin Hewick, who was making an album entitled *From Brussels With Love*. These first actions were very low key, in keeping with the decision to start anew. A group just forming would not be granted huge amounts of press coverage, and they felt that it would be mercenary of them to benefit from the Joy Division legacy. "We just wanted to take it easy," Rob Gretton said, "to work out what we were going to do." They also wanted time to themselves, to remember Ian and heal the wounds caused by his death. The trio's "début" concert, on July 29, 1980, at Manchester's Beach club, was done entirely without publicity or warning. They didn't even tell the band who they wanted to open for them that they were coming!

As Gretton remembered, "We actually planned it. I remember A Certain Ratio were a little surprised when we showed up as their support." Fans who noticed "Joy Division" stencilled on the equipment cases heard instrumental versions of the still-unnamed trio's new repertoire. They'd had their coming-out party. Now it was time for them to slowly reclaim their throne.

They chose a name in August. Many silly ones were put up to vote and dismissed, including The Hit, The Eternal, Stevie and the J.D.'s, Sunshine Valley Dance Band, and Witch Doctors of Zimbabwe. At the time, Rob Gretton was reading a book of essays by the Situationist political movement entitled *Leaving the Twentieth Century*, and a passage about a "new order of architecture" stuck in his mind. "At the time, I thought it was a very neutral name," he said. He mentioned the phrase "new order" during a band meeting, and the musicians fell in love with it. Weren't they the New Order of Joy Division? The name had been used before, by a punk band doing business as the New Order, and like Warsaw and Joy Division, the title had links with Fascism. Adolf Hitler envisioned a New Order of mankind, with the Aryan race ruling the Earth. The band was willing to ignore this connotation, preferring to focus on what it meant with reference to Joy Division. They would be called New Order. And the outside world would often be startled, angered, and upset by their choice of name. The Nazi rumours which were born when Barney wore an armband and shouted about Rudolf Hess on the Electric Circus stage would not retire with the Joy Division name.

The cancellation of Joy Division's tour had disappointed many American fans, and New Order resolved to make it up to them by touring the US with A Certain Ratio. The trip was preceded by two more unadvertised gigs and the American release of Joy Division's 'She's Lost Control (Version)', a remix of the *Unknown Pleasures* track, backed with 'Atmosphere', finally available in unlimited numbers. The colour sleeve by Peter Saville depicted a forest in winter, unavoidably suggesting coldness and death. British demand for this record was so strong that Factory eventually released it in the UK with the song order reversed. Joy Division were gone, but not forgotten.

New Order's first American concert took place at Maxwell's in Hoboken, New Jersey, on Friday, September 20, 1980, and they spent the following Monday and Tuesday at Eastern Artists Recording Studio taping 'Ceremony' and 'In A Lonely Place', with Martin Hannett producing. When the session was complete, they rode back to their Manhattan hotel to get some sleep, only to wake up the next morning and discover thieves had stolen their van and all the instruments it contained! The heist forced them to reschedule their concerts as they ran around, renting and buying guitars and drums, not fully re-outfitted until Friday, when they played Hurrah in New York City.

Joy Division had planned to begin their tour at Hurrah, so there was considerable excitement at the gig. Among the fans present was a young film-maker named Michael Shamberg. "I was introduced to A Certain Ratio," Shamberg said, "and I made a short film with them. That's how I met Tony Wilson and New Order. I made a tape of New Order's concert, gave Rob Gretton a copy because he requested it, and Tony Wilson liked it a lot." Wilson liked it so much that he asked Shamberg to continue to work with Factory by producing the label's videos. Within a year, the company established an American branch called Of Factory New York, with Shamberg managing and promoting New Order to a larger audience.

Right: Gillian on stage at the Felt Forum In New York.

The US tour exposed a big problem for New Order, the necessity of having a lead singer. As Gretton said, "They all gave it a try, but everyone had trouble playing at the same time." Additionally, Hooky had a disruptive tendency of turning his back on the audience, and Steve had no stage presence when hidden behind a drum kit. Barney seemed like the best candidate for vocalist. They decided to get a fourth member to relieve him of some of his musical responsibilities, but didn't want anyone with a seasoned, distinct style of their own who might unduly influence the band. They also wanted a person they'd known for a long time. All eyes fell on Gillian Gilbert.

Gillian, Stephen Morris' soft-spoken, burgundy-haired girlfriend, lived in Peel Green near Macclesfield. She had gone to school with Steve's sister, dabbled in music as a part of the all-girl Inadequates, and was now studying graphic design at Stockport Technical College. Basically inexperienced as a musician, she passed a cursory audition and became New Order's second guitarist/keyboardist/vocalist, shifting the instrumental workload from Barney, who became the lead singer. Gillian's first New Order gig took place at the Squat in Manchester, where Steve's song 'Procession' also débuted.

'Procession' was the first New Order composition not to closely imitate the Joy Division sound. Heavily computerised, relaxed and pretty, its lyrics were dreamy and thoughtful, but not depressing. Perhaps the credit for this belonged to Gillian. Her participation in the band alleviated much stress, and her refreshing sense of wonder kept everyone busy teaching her recording techniques, thus taking their minds off Ian's death. By early December, she was proving herself to be a vital member of New Order, and participated in a re-recording of 'Ceremony', this one livelier, faster, and better than the original.

New Order performed all around England and Scotland at the start of 1981, also recording guitar overdubs for versions of Joy Division's 'The Kill' and 'The Only Mistake', intended as part of a forthcoming collection of unreleased songs. On the 26th of January they were in the studio again, recording a session at John Peel's request. The same Tony Wilson who'd produced Joy Division's last Peel Session worked on this one, helping New Order record 'Truth', 'Senses', 'Dreams Never End', and 'ICB', the last title often rumoured among fans to stand for "Ian Curtis Buried." But the failure of the session as a whole was New Order's inability to bury the Joy Division sound. Ian's lyrics influenced Barney's, but Barney couldn't sing of manna falling from heaven with the same convincing authority. He was trying to sound like someone else, which was the same problem Warsaw had suffered under before the band found their identity. Barney's failures at school had whittled away his self-confidence, and he hesitated to express his true feelings in his songs. 'ICB', meanwhile, actually used a drum pattern similar to the one used for 'Atrocity Exhibition.' The Peel Session would satisfy some degree of the public's hunger for New Order music, but the band's best work obviously lay ahead of them.

The band remained trapped in their Joy Division mode while working on a first LP, *Movement*. All four Peel Session songs, as well as several more, were recorded under Martin Hannett's guidance. None of them besides the album's opening cut, 'Dreams Never End', truly distinguished themselves. 'Dreams...' stood apart mostly because Peter Hook sang lead vocals, and the sentiments it expressed recalled the feistiness of 'Ceremony'. But all other tracks on *Movement* lacked any sense of personality, and the strain of recording them tried the band members' friendships with Martin Hannett and each other.

On 'Dreams Never End', Hooky's fuzzy basslines and multi-tracked vocals, as well as Barney and Gillian's guitar work, offered delights behind Stephen's overpowering drumbeats. The lyrics, especially a promise of, "No looking back now", alerted the audience that this band desperately wanted to overcome the horrors of their past.

They wished to overcome the horrors of their past, but could not, or would not, abandon their old styles of performance. For example, Barney sang 'Truth' in an Ian-esque monotone to a zombie-like church organ accompaniment. The result was a sub-Joy Division hodgepodge which offered neither truth nor entertainment. Hannett whipped out special effects for the rhythm tracks of 'Senses', trying to spice up the otherwise bland composition. His studio tricks could often intensify the strengths of a good song, but they were unable to hide the weaknesses of a bad one. The live drums and ambling bass of 'Chosen Time' worked quite nicely together, redeeming the end of side one, but the studied melancholia of 'ICB' launched side two on a weak note.

'The Him' – or, perhaps, as it should have been titled, 'The Hymn' – might have functioned best as an instrumental evocation of the stifling quality of organised religion. Barney's often incomprehensible lyrics detracted from the track as a whole. Ecclesiastical images such as, "White circles, black lines surround me," offered cryptic hints of the singer's intentions. His shyness, which reduced him to mumbling vague statements, prevented him from giving his ideas the forum they required.

Hooky and Gillian duetted on 'Doubts Even Here', a slowly-developing, menacing poem which, like most of the tracks on *Movement*, hid lyrics behind a wall of sound. One of the few lines at the Coda which could be understood said, "Don't throw our joy away". This could have been addressed to Ian Curtis as much as anyone. The loss of the man's friendship, and his master's touch at songwriting, influenced *Movement* to the core.

'Denial' featured Barney's admission of being trapped, "In a house full of doors and no exits." Fear of the unknown was that prison; fear of New Order breaking free of the suffocating safety of imitating Joy Division. They would have to break away from that prison by establishing their own identities.

As New Order struggled with their album, Factory released the band's début single, the American recordings of 'Ceremony' and 'In A Lonely Place'. This was the first New Order project to get widespread attention – the Peel Session had not yet been broadcast – and the primary difference between this band and Joy Division lay in Barney's faltering vocals. His voice may have cracked, but his guitar playing rivalled the best he'd ever done. 'Ceremony' was a winner, appealing to over a hundred thousand record buyers who purchased the disc in such quantities that it went to No. 34 on the charts. The dirge on the flipside, however, sounded as if it had been recorded at the wrong speed, and the lyric, "cord stretches tight, then it breaks", seemed in bad taste, even though Ian Curtis had written it. Only Stephen Morris' shimmering drumwork redeemed the track.

New Order returned to London on February 9 to finish mixing its Peel Session and perform at the popular "ultradisco", Heaven. Martin Hannett mixed the concert's quadraphonic sound, and Paul Morley had the usual complimentary things to say about the band he'd championed since Day One. Yet most reports of this first major English gig were mixed, citing stage fright and uncertainty as the overwhelming factors propelling New Order's show. The loss of Ian Curtis' commanding presence left them without a showman to entertain the crowd. All New Order would offer was music. They were too nervous, and Barney too inexperienced at interacting with audiences, for them to put on a "show". This offended much of the public, who thought the band were simply ignoring them. New Order got a reputation for being cold onstage.

New Order spent March recording 'Procession' and the equally futuristic 'Everything's Gone Green', and dedicated April to touring Scotland. On May 6, they returned to London, playing before 3,000 fans at the Forum Ballroom while many more stood outside the venue without tickets. The group quickly arranged a follow-up gig at the Talbot Tabernacle so that everyone locked out of the Forum could see the band in concert. New Order might not have paid much attention to their audiences while they were on stage, but they certainly cared about them nevertheless.

During the last part of May, the band travelled across Europe, playing in Paris, Brussels, Hamburg, Copenhagen, Stockholm, Goteborg, Oslo, and Berlin. They returned to the UK for a gig at the Glastonbury Fayre outdoor festival on June 20, their largest audience to date. A silver-coloured pyramid loomed above the stage, Tony Wilson captured New Order's every move on videotape for use in a home movie project, and Barney, overwhelmed and intoxicated, collapsed. "I made the film for myself, really," Wilson said. "I made a nice little piece out of it, as well. It was two songs, some Shakespeare, there was some documentary, it was a nice little ten-minute package. It was quite fun. It's a nice record of the time; it showed New Order were actually much more lively and vibrant than the *Movement* album might suggest." Shortly after this gig, the re-recorded 'Ceremony' was released, Gillian's vinyl début.

Near the end of August 1981, rumours began to circulate that New Order were breaking up. Peter Hook went so far as to say he was leaving, in order to become manager of the band Stockholm Monsters, while Barney Albrecht was reportedly being thrown out for "overacting" on stage. Happily, a split didn't occur, and New Order released a single to cure everyone's summertime blues.

'Procession' b/w 'Everything's Gone Green' came out in early September, and without any promotion and very little airplay, climbed to number 38 on the British chart. The logo for New Order's publishing company Be Music (as in "bemused music") appeared on the label, and it rekindled the undying Nazi hype when people mistook Saville's flowing "B" design for a German "SS". The bandmembers all had a favourite shade they wanted Factory to use on the one-colour sleeve, so the company decided to make everybody happy (and collectors perplexed) by issuing nine covers, all in different tones.

Still, a double album set of Joy Division outtakes and live material débuted on John Peel's Radio One show and was issued through Factory in October. Peter Saville wanted all the copies to come in a cloth sleeve, rather than the standard cardboard, to make *Still* resemble a hardbound book. Unfortunately, the cost of manufacturing the package this way taxed the resources of Factory. Tony Wilson explained, "Saville says, 'Ah, I've got this great fucking idea,' and I go, 'Yeah? Yeah? Yeah? What's it going to cost?' And he goes, 'Uh...' By then it was too late, cost Factory about eight quid each." Future printings of *Still* came in a "softcover" cardboard

edition, the clothbound first run of ten thousand trading hands at high prices in the used record market. Some critics viewed *Still* as a greedy move intended to milk Joy Division fans out of money by selling material the band never thought was worth releasing in the first place, while others recognised it as Factory's attempt to offer an inexpensive alternative to the bootleg Joy Division records being produced by anonymous manufacturers. "There's been a row over the years," Wilson laughed, "I thought *Still* was a bit boring and a bit stupid, somehow. I never really liked it. It was more of an accounting exercise, getting all of the old tracks out." The fans appreciated the gesture; they boosted *Still* to number five on the charts.

New Order toured the US as *Still* was released, and Michael Shamberg recounted the events leading up to one of the band's New York gigs: "New Order were supposed to play at this little club down on Broadway and Houston, but that little club got squeezed out of existence by local competition (New York at the time suffered from a "club war", with different venues trying to dominate the scene). The Peppermint Lounge tried to book New Order for the empty night, and I called the band and said, 'Listen, let's do our own show somewhere.' And they were into it, so we found the Ukranian National Home."

Being a cultural centre, like the Russel Club in England, the Ukranian National Home was an unusual location for a rock concert. However, this quirkiness added to the venue's appeal as far as the band was concerned. They decided to film the gig, so Shamberg contacted his friend Barry Rebo to co-produce the taping. "He came in," Shamberg said, "and just put up everything because he was interested. He shot the band with his own camera crew, directing them on the spot. The show was great, and that was how I got to really start working with New Order."

The highlight of the Ukranian National Home gig was the performance of a new song entitled 'Taboo Number 7', later known as 'Temptation'. Barney created lyrics on the spot, and as Tony Wilson observed, this unrehearsed vocal allowed the singer to express his own feelings, as opposed to deliberately imitating Ian Curtis. "On that (video) you have a very early version of 'Temptation.' He's struggling to find the words, and in a nonsense verse, 'You've got green eyes, you've got blue eyes, you've got grey eyes,' in that nonsense repetition, suddenly Barney finds his voice." Just as 'Novelty' allowed Warsaw to break away from the pack, 'Taboo Number 7/Temptation' distinguished New Order from Joy Division.

The band came home in late November, finally seeing *Movement*, which had also been released during the tour. Few people liked it, including New Order, and Tony Wilson may have described the record best when he said, "*Movement* was Barney trying to write lyrics like Ian, the group trying to play like Joy Division, and Martin Hannett's relationship with the group finally crumbling. So *Movement* was a great disappointment.

"Martin Hannett had feelings that it was time to move on. What happened then was a great big row erupted, with *Movement* as the background, between Hannett and his partners in Factory. He was suing us and taking us to High Court, trying to close the record company down. We had two years of very unpleasant litigation and fighting." Martin Hannett had been one of five Factory directors, along with Tony Wilson, Rob Gretton, Alan Erasmus, and Peter Saville. Hannett sold his share for forty thousand pounds, giving Wilson 32%, Gretton 31%, Erasmus 31% and Saville 6% of the company. This cleared Factory of any further legal entanglements with Hannett, but left New Order without a producer. Having produced their own demos, and knowing better than anyone else how they wished to sound, the band saw only one option: they'd produce themselves.

New Order + Joy Division

Quite a few holiday gifts were available to New Order's supporters at the end of 1981. Factory Benelux, a secondary company located in Belgium, served as a clearing house for leftover tracks, and it released a 12" featuring 'Everything's Gone Green' b/w 'Cries And Whispers' (named for the Ingmar Bergman film) and 'Mesh', as well as 'The Factory Compilation' videocassette, which included live renditions of 'Everything's Gone Green' and 'Truth' from New Order's Brussels gig. And if that wasn't enough, the entire group appeared on ITV's *Granada Reports*, all dressed as Santa Claus!

On January 4, 1982, New Order filmed a concert before a studio audience for broadcast on BBC-TV's *Riverside*, and spent the next five days recording two of the songs they'd performed, the high-tech 'Hurt' (introduced by a robotic voice counting into the song, "One, two, three, four!") and 'Taboo Number 7', now officially retitled 'Temptation'. The lyrics to the latter were unapologetically gushy; 'Temptation' was a love song full of jangly guitars, pounding electronic drums, and Gillian's gorgeous keyboard lines. Barney sang many of the lyrics he'd improvised at the Ukranian National Home without a trace of irony or bitterness, as he may have been wont to do if he'd stuck to emulating Ian. When the songs appeared on vinyl in March, the 7" had a message etched between the runout grooves of the record and the label which read, "Try listening to the 12"," and the 12", which featured a more guitar-heavy 'Temptation' and an extended 'Hurt' asking, "What do you think?" Inexplicably, 'Temptation' stalled at a disappointing No. 29 on the UK chart, perhaps due to Peter Saville's decision to reverse-emboss the titles on the cover without making them easily legible. Tony Wilson lamented 'Temptation's' relative failure on the charts, and for years championed it as a lost classic.

The band embarked on another European tour in April '82. While most audiences accepted short concerts as New Order's prerogative, the crowd at the Glazenzaal in Rotterdam felt cheated when the band walked offstage after playing for only forty-five minutes. New Order's policy of doing ten songs per night allowed them to constantly change their set list and keep concerts from becoming repetitive, but the Dutch fans threw bottles at the roadies in protest: they had spent a lot of money on tickets, and felt the concert should have been longer. A riot broke out, and as usual, Peter Hook entered the fray with both hands swinging. This time, however, he encountered a New Order "fan" strong enough to punch back and stun him. Roadies carried Hook backstage, and a hastily-devised refund policy allowed people in Holland to obtain a refund if they thought a ten-song gig wasn't long enough. After two concerts in Belgium, New Order flew home to work on their next big project, the opening of their very own club which they called the Hacienda.

A boat showroom had closed on 11-13 Whitworth Street in Manchester, and New Order envisioned it as the location of a new dance hall. They remembered their Warsaw days of not getting booked for concerts, and saw the establishment of a fresh venue – a sort of Factory Club, Mark 2 – as an aid to struggling young bands. New Order and Factory Records purchased the building together, remodelled the interior, installed the proper lighting and sound equipment, put in a bar, and on May 21, opened the Hacienda, Manchester's newest nightspot. Architect Ben Kelly designed the interior, covering the I-beams which supported the roof with yellow and black safety stripes to reinforce the "Factory" look.

Tony Wilson said the Hacienda was intended, "as a club, a space, which could be a venue, could be a disco, could be anything. It holds thirteen-hundred people. But the business side of running the Hacienda became an absolute nightmare. We believed it would cost a quarter of a million pounds to get started, but it turned out to be a million-pound diversification. The secret of expanding business is choosing a good lieutenant, and the lieutenant we chose to run the Hacienda was a complete idiot. After two years we replaced him with a committee of good people, and a committee of good people is like one, great big idiot. It cost a fortune in taxes, and to keep it going, we all had to fucking kill ourselves. We all suffered deprivations." For Tony Wilson, this meant pumping all of the income he earned from Factory into the Hacienda, and for New Order, it would mean near-constant touring in the years to come. Much of the money they earned off *Movement* was also siphoned into the club. "New Order made a lot of money out of going to America and touring," Wilson said. "If they hadn't done that, they'd be penniless because of the problems with the Hacienda."

New Order launched the Hacienda with a party and the début of a twenty-one minute recording of Stephen Morris playing the synthesizer entitled 'Prime 5.8.6.', the name being a joke: "five ate six." Then they mailed John Peel a ready-made session featuring '5.8.6.' (an abbreviated version of 'Prime' with instruments and vocals added), a meditative cover version of the reggae track 'Turn The Heater On' by Keith Hudson, the jazzy 'We All Stand', and the languid 'Too Late'. The session confirmed what 'Temptation' and 'Hurt' had suggested: New Order were blending electronic and acoustic instruments, perhaps not always successfully, but certainly bravely. Most other bands would've restricted themselves to just one genre or the other. New Order had created a sound all their own.

Most of the summer of 1982 was devoted to live shows: a one-off in Finland, an Italian tour where the promoter forced New Order to do encores, a free gig at the Hacienda to attract new club members, a show at the Venue in Blackpool, and headlining spots at the Futurama Sci-Fi and Independent Rock and Roll festivals. Films of New Order performing 'Ceremony', 'In A Lonely Place', and the uncredited 'Prime 5.8.6.' were included on the 'A Factory Video' home cassette, and Barney snuck away from New Order long enough to contribute synthesizers to disco singles by Factory labelmates 52nd Street: 'Look Into My Eyes' b/w 'Express', and 'Twice As Nice' b/w 'Cool As Ice'.

Factory released a video companion to *Still* in August. The tape 'Here Are The Young Men' was originally intended to compile all of Joy Division's TV appearances, but the BBC and ITV wanted too much money to licence the films. The footage eventually used came from Richard Boon's home movies of Joy Division at the Manchester Apollo, 8mm shorts of Joy Division in Holland, photographs taken at the opening of Plan K, and the 'Love Will Tear Us Apart' promo. Once again, fans were delighted to receive previously unreleased Joy Division material, and once again, the critics accused Factory of trying to make money by selling a bootleg-quality patchwork of outtakes. "The actual quality is not that great," Rob Gretton admitted, "but it's nice to have." In a magnanimous gesture, Factory added a disclaimer permitting fans to duplicate 'Here Are The Young Men' on a non-profit basis, and New Order reserved a Factory catalogue number for their own eventual video retrospective: 'Here Are The Old Men'.

By mid-November, New Order had recorded three complete new songs; the melancholy 'Only The Lonely', later re-named 'Leave Me Alone', a sophisticated reworking of '5.8.6.' called 'Blue Monday', and an instrumental entitled 'Murder', which featured dialogue lifted from the band's favourite movies, including *2001: A Space Odyssey*. These tracks reflected a growing interest in dance music, especially New York's rap/hip-hop movement. This infatuation led Rob Gretton to call Michael Shamberg late one night, asking on behalf of the band, "Do you know anything about this guy Arthur Baker?" It was a name they'd seen on many dance records in their collections.

"Well," Shamberg said, "he's a record producer who's worked on a lot of hip-hop stuff. His partner's John Robie; I met Robie when we did a remix of Cabaret Voltaire's 'Yashar.'"

"New Order wants Baker to remix '5.8.6.'," Gretton said. "Could you see if he's interested?"

"Sure."

Shamberg got in touch with Baker, who, as it turned out, was very interested: he was a New Order fan! Baker and the group compared schedules and made plans for a collaboration.

Since North American listeners usually paid high prices for New Order records imported from Europe, the inexpensive '1981-1982' retrospective EP was released in the US and Canada for their benefit. Although missing 'In A Lonely Place', 'Cries And Whispers', and both versions of 'Ceremony', '1981-1982' did include 'Everything's Gone Green', 'Procession', 'Mesh', and the 12" versions of 'Hurt' and 'Temptation'. It was a great sampler, just the thing for casual fans to listen to.

Meanwhile, New Order touched down in Melbourne on a jumbo jet, all ready to tour Australia and New Zealand. They were in for a big surprise, however, when they stepped off the plane after a thirty-six hour trip and were sprayed with disinfectant! "That's great", Stephen Morris thought. "'Welcome to our country, don't spread any diseases.' Wow."

Starting on November 25 at the Palais Theatre in Melbourne, New Order wound through Sydney, Auckland, Wellington, Christchurch, and Perth. As this was nearly the height of summer, the band spent lots of time on Bondi Beach, and were soon as bronzed and tanned as the Aussies. Zipping back to England in December, they finished their holiday shopping and intended to fly to New York to work with Arthur Baker on '5.8.6.', but decided they ought to finish recording their second album instead. Staying in Manchester, they pressed a flexi-disc of Christmas songs they'd recorded the year before – 'Rocking Carol' and Beethoven's 'Freude Schoner Gotterfunken' – and gave them away to anyone spending Christmas Eve at the Hacienda.

In January 1983, New Order drove to Pink Floyd's Britannia Row studios in London and mixed their second album, at various times titled

Fuck, Piss Off You Lot, and *How Does It Feel*. Barney's lyrics for the LP were really good, thanks to his new habit of transcribing ad-libbed vocal performances and embellishing them late at night, without anyone or anything to distract him. He'd freewrite in a very unselfconscious way, words and melodies seeming to flow through him without effort. He reasoned that he had gained this ability as a result of people thinking and dreaming about New Order, with his brain receiving their thoughts. A lot of sceptics raised an eyebrow when they heard that theory, but there was no denying that the method had produced New Order's best work to date.

It began with 'Age Of Consent', an infectious commentary to a departed love. "I've lost you, I've lost you, I've lost you, I've lost you, I've lost you," Barney cried, then Hook's bass and Gillian's synthesizer intimated a feeling of nostalgia. 'We All Stand' loped along like a sleepy pony, but 'The Village', a jolly number with a catchy chorus and memorable Hook bassline, restored the album to an upbeat pace. Into this festive mood Barney stuck what may have been a reference to Ian and Debbie Curtis: "Their love died three years ago, unspoken words they cannot show." The shock of this lyric matched the herky-jerky transition into '5.8.6,' the music during the segue sounding a bit too slow and slightly out of tune. When Barney sang of, "these feelings I can't hide", he seemed to describe how freewriting had unleashed his muse. His personality, as well as his bandmates', was evident all through this LP. The music was refreshingly removed from the Joy Division imitations on *Movement*.

Gillian played a sad tune for 'Your Silent Face', which the band labelled a Kraftwerk ripoff. They would often refer to this song as 'KW-1'; the first Kraftwerk knock-off they had written that week. Barney sang some of his most evocative lyrics on 'Your Silent Face', including the immortal, "You've caught me at a bad time, so why don't you piss off." This certainly was not Joy Division.

'Ultraviolence' got its title from a slang term in the book and film *A Clockwork Orange*, which the four cinema buffs in New Order must have seen. Barney's lyrics for 'Ultraviolence' were vague, and on the heavily-processed 'Ecstasy', they were unintelligible. The band returned to their acoustic roots for 'Leave Me Alone', the album's melancholy finale. Its gentleness and simplicity were endearing, leaving the listener with a warm glow. Moving back and forth between electronic and traditional instruments, New Order employed any tool necessary to express their emotions. Their musical and lyrical vocabularies had grown a thousandfold.

At long last, they flew to Manhattan to work with Arthur Baker. He still expected to produce '5.8.6.' as he and the band originally intended, but New Order now wanted him to work on 'Blue Monday'. They eventually agreed to write a song together, but since the band weren't used to working as quickly as Baker, New Order were paralysed by in-the-studio culture shock. They only had a week to record something, and kept drawing a blank, walking around in circles asking, "Isn't it time to go home, yet?" Desperate, they shaped a guitar lick from Hot Chocolate's 'Emmaline' into an instantly accessible love song in the electronic/acoustic mode of 'Temptation', and named it 'Thieves Like Us', after a 1974 gangster movie starring Keith Carradine and Shelly Duvall. Then, armed with a seven-minute drum track that Baker already had on tape, they wrote the discoey 'Confusion': certainly the best word to sum up their stay in New York.

New Order said goodbye to Baker, both parties happy and open to future collaborations. They got home in time for the March 9, 1983 release of 'Blue Monday' backed with a dub version entitled 'The Beach'. The songs were intended to be very mechanical and anonymous, hence the lack of a readable band name or title on the cover (Saville had translated both into a colour code printed along the side of the imitation floppy disc sleeve). The cuts were driven by an aggressive disco beat which seduced clubgoers everywhere. 'Blue Monday' was easily the most exciting and liberating record to come out since The Sex Pistols' 'God Save The Queen', because it inspired thousands of young people who loved the exuberance of disco and the brute force of rock to try their own hand at mixing the two styles together. Up until 'Blue Monday' the whole genre known as "synthesizer music" as performed by keyboard-only groups like Orchestral Manoeuvres In The Dark and Human League, was looked down upon as passionless and wimpy. Peter Hook's bass riffs in 'Blue Monday', performed alongside Gillian Gilbert's keyboard lines, pointed the way towards a new order of dance music. Just as The Sex Pistols had brought wonder and excitement into the lives of New Order, New Order were passing those gifts along to the youth of the world. They'd paid back their debt to music.

The lyrics to 'Blue Monday' were captivating, but also ambiguous. People tried to decipher them in many ways, usually in a military context. But Barney's improvised words seemed to especially invoke Monday, May 19, 1980, the day Joy Division were to depart for America, when the "ship in the harbour"– success – was spoiled by "your misfortune" – Ian's suicide. Was 'The Beach' a silly reference to the Beach club? Barney wouldn't say if his lyrics were intended as a message to Ian, but fans didn't mind. All told, 'Blue Monday' sold an incredible seven hundred and fifty thousand units worldwide, became a Top Ten hit in England, introduced New Order to millions of new people, influenced a whole new generation of musicians, and raised enough cash to continue to keep the Hacienda solvent. Not bad for a song originally composed to try out a new drum machine!

The British sales of half a million copies of 'Blue Monday' should have earned New Order a gold record from the British Phonograph Institute, but the band were ineligible to receive one because Factory was not a BPI member. Tony Wilson felt the band deserved some kind of trophy for their accomplishment, so he said, "We made heavy bronze statuettes with the corporate logo and '(the 'Blue Monday' catalogue number) Fac 73 – 500,000' stamped in. So everyone (in New Order) got one of these bronze fucking things." Malcolm Whitehead and Stephen Morris produced a computer-animated video for the song, which was eventually featured on the Factory home video 'Shorts'.

Not long after the release of 'Blue Monday', New Order played a date at Kingston Polytechnic's Rag Ball at the Tolworth Recreation Centre, and the chaotic gig was one of the maddest the band had ever performed. Their newfound success attracted many young people who went bonkers on the dance floor, eventually crushing anyone standing by the front of the stage. By the fourth song, Barney announced, "Listen, you (the crowd) had better move back, right, 'cause a lot of people are getting hurt." The audience still refused to calm down, leading Barney to call them "bollock-brains", and Peter Hook to warn that the roadies would, "rip your fucking heads off," if the throng didn't settle. New Order felt the audience did not deserve an encore, but performed one anyway, explaining, "The door (leading offstage) is jammed and we cannot get out." By the time their final song had ended, the exit had been coaxed loose and New Order escaped.

Their second LP was released directly after a tour of Ireland and Scotland. *Power, Corruption and Lies,* named after a sentence on the back cover of a paperback edition of George Orwell's *1984,* appeared in stores on May 3rd, 1983. Its design was characteristically subdued; a painting by

Henri Fantin-Latour on the front, and a pseudo floppy-disc design à la 'Blue Monday' on the back. Saville seemed to suggest that art of the future would be created on computers, rather than on three-dimensional surfaces, in keeping with New Order's increasingly synthetic sound.

The circle on the back of *Power, Corruption and Lies* was the long-awaited codebreaker for the coloured blocks that appeared on the side of 'Blue Monday' and this album. Starting at the top of the circle (the equivalent of "12 o'clock"), the solid green wedge stood for "A", the solid yellow for "B", and so on, until the yellow and pink wedge, which stood for "Z". The real numbers one through nine could be deciphered the same way: solid green for "1", solid yellow for "2", up to solid blue for "9". Silver octagons represented spaces between words. Employing this system, the front cover of the LP read "FACT 75" (the catalogue number), and the two sides of the inside cover read, "NEW ORDER POWER CORRUTIRN (sic) AND LIES." Judging by this "spelling error", even Peter Saville hadn't mastered his own secret code! The 'Blue Monday' sleeve could now be deciphered to read, "FAC 73 BLUE MONDAY AND THE BEACH NEW ORDER". The album reached number four on the UK chart despite this consumer-unfriendly packaging (remember, the titles did not appear in standard English), and in North America, distributors Rough Trade stickered the album to inform people that this was, in fact, the New Order release they'd been searching for.

The Hacienda continued to suck money from Factory and the band, so New Order scheduled an overdue three-week tour of the US and Canada, where *Power, Corruption and Lies* and 'Blue Monday' had become favourites on new wave and college radio stations. One of two British warm-up gigs fell on Rob Gretton's birthday, so as a gift to him, New Order performed 'Love Will Tear Us Apart'. The delighted audience was in shock, for New Order had never played a Joy Division song before, and might never do so again. They hadn't fully recovered from Ian's death, yet this public attempt to heal did much to help the band overcome the loss.

New Order's tour began in June and included stops in Georgia, Texas, California, Vancouver, Minnesota, Illinois, Michigan, Montreal, New York, the District of Columbia, and New Jersey. Along the way, the band met with reporters – this seemed like as good a time as any to re-open communications and see if the state of things had improved – but as one former employee Of Factory New York said, "I'd take anything New Order say to the press with a grain of salt." The group were not opposed to embellishing stories, just to keep the public from knowing their true opinions. And sometimes, New Order remained shrouded in mystery through no effort of their own. A photographer from a major US entertainment publication arrived at New York's Paradise Garage club to take a picture of the band. An employee told him he could find New Order on the roof, but when he got there, all that he found were what looked like a bunch of tourists. After a brief wait, he left without any photographs, never realising that the clutch of people wearing Bermuda shorts and sipping drinks were New Order, whom he probably expected to be dressed in slacks and ties. The Joy Division look had been discarded. Barney and Hooky had streaked their hair with Sun-In. New Order were willing to go casual. They were no longer obsessed with the heart of darkness.

Tony Wilson and Michael Shamberg filmed the Paradise Garage concert for use in an upcoming video of 'Confusion'. According to Wilson, "The problem with every New Order video is deciding what to do with the band, because they don't want to mime, don't want to act, and just don't want to make videos. At some point I'd been talking to Arthur Baker in his studio, and at about one in the morning he said, 'Hold on,' and took a mix he'd done of some group off the tape machine. He led me to the Funhouse

disco, put the mix into the machine at the side of the D.J. booth, played the track, watched the kids dancing to it, thought, 'Needs more hi-hat,' got back in his car, and went back to the studio. I watched that and thought, 'That's really wild, that's wonderful, that's nice.' So in my mind was that story."

Michael Shamberg was thinking along the same lines, having just read an article about the Funhouse in the *Village Voice*. "It was about John 'Jellybean' Benitez being the club's D.J., Arthur Baker and John Robie going there to play tapes to the kids, the whole hip-hop scene. But the article was really about seeing that place and that lifestyle through this one girl, a day in her life. She'd get up, work in a pizza parlour, then go to Manhattan in the evening as part of a dance group called The Juice Crew. She was dancing at the Funhouse, took it very seriously, and that was her fun."

These two sources became the basis for the video. Shamberg said "The storyline was Arthur Baker in the studio mixing 'Confusion,' going down to the Funhouse to play it, listen to it, and get a reaction, the band performing at the Paradise Garage, coming offstage, meeting Arthur Baker and Jellybean in the Funhouse, and this girl, played by Elise Bitic, and her life: working, going home and changing her clothes, meeting her friends as part of The Juice Crew, performing out on the dancefloor of the Funhouse, everyone in the booth watching, and the celebration of the song. That's where the video came from." "We created something that would naturally happen," Wilson said. "We shot it with a friend of ours who lived with us at the time named Charlie Sturridge, who made the *Brideshead Revisited* television series."

'Confusion' was released as a 12" single in August, through Factory in England and Arthur Baker's Streetwise label in America. The record presented four different remixes of the basic track: 'Confusion', 'Confused Beats', an instrumental version and 'Confusion (Rough Mix)', which had been premièred at the New Music Seminar. The song became very popular in discos. Between the successes of 'Blue Monday' and now 'Confusion', New Order were acquiring a reputation as a great disco act. Much of the credit must go to Baker; it was his production that made 'Confusion' so catchy. But ironically, his production was a point of contention between him and the band. New Order wished he had chosen the arrangement they used when performing 'Confusion' in concert, instead of the more accessible one he did pick. Even if the band didn't like Baker's production, the public did, buying so many copies that the song went to No.12 in England.

Around the same time, Factory issued a videocassette of New Order's Ukranian National Home gig entitled 'Taras Shevchenko', after the nineteenth-century Ukranian poet and political activist. Some critics were disappointed, referring to the band's lack of stage presence as a major flaw in their performance. New Order were obviously suffering from camera shyness, which intensified their natural tendency to be introverted. Michael Shamberg described 'Taras Shevchenko' best as, "an intimate portrait" of the band, just spreading their wings and learning to fly. The video for 'Confusion' was added to the end, showing how much the band had loosened up in two years' time.

Solo projects dominated New Order's fall and winter, all the band-members working under the alias Be Music. Barney, who in the spring had produced two versions of the bouncy 'Love Tempo' for Manchester's Quando Quango with help from his new buddy, Johnny Marr of The Smiths, worked on the single 'Looking From A Hilltop' by Section 25. Steve and Gillian (as well as one of Gillian's relatives, Kim Gilbert) collaborated with Michael Shamberg's girlfriend Stanton Miranda as members of her group Thick Pigeon. The fruit of their labours was the delightful, avant-garde

Johnny Marr.

LP *Two Crazy Cowboys*, issued through Of Factory New York in a weird die-cut sleeve. Gillian got to sing more than her usual share with New Order, and the album – fairly obscure and rare – rewarded the curious New Order fans who tracked it down. The Steve and Gillian tag-team also produced a record by The Life, and may have been the mystery producers of 'Deep Sleep', 'Lost Again' and 'Wave' by the Factory band Red Turns Too... Hooky stuck with his friends The Stockholm Monsters, mixing sound at their live shows and producing one of their singles, as well as discs by Nyam Nyam and La Volta La Kota, whose bandmember Dave Hicks was a good friend. New Order regrouped for some concerts in December, but spent most of the winter alone.

At the end of January, 1984, the band got a little publicity in the mainstream American press. *Newsweek* magazine's cover story, "Britain Rocks America – Again", mentioned New Order as one of several, "savvy and sometimes sinister names that conjure up a strange new world of pop." New Order already had a cult audience in the US, but even national coverage like this couldn't get them into all the country's record stores and radio stations. Of Factory New York and Rough Trade simply didn't have the resources to promote the band as much as they deserved. Everyone seemed to like New Order once they heard them, but without widespread airplay and distribution, the group would have to be satisfied with earning fans one by one. Major labels offered large amounts of money and the complete efforts of their publicity staffs, but nobody, it seemed, would offer the creative control the band enjoyed under Factory. Unwilling to compromise their art for financial success, they stoically remained independent.

'Thieves Like Us' and 'Lonesome Tonight', two irresistible studies of the power of love, were released together on a 12" single in March, 1984. The songs boasted many comforting sentiments, but one of the most human parts of 'Thieves Like Us' came after the final verse, when Barney could be heard clearing his throat in the studio and spitting on the floor, a funny, affecting touch which most bands never would have left in. Errors like this tore down the barriers between the band and their audience. New Order never professed to being special, and they were willing to

expose all sides of their personalities, including the embarrassing, imperfect ones. As such, their music became more impressive than it would have been had they polished over all the faults. Photographer Trevor Key's calm still-life on the cover reflected the stark beauty of the songs, which critics and the public embraced whole-heartedly. The disc went to No. 18 in the UK.

Three months later, New Order followed this up with the demoniac, minimalist 'Murder', a genuinely scary instrumental occasionally interrupted by the gibbering of *2001: A Space Odyssey*'s Hal the Computer. The B-side was an instrumental remix of 'Thieves Like Us', even more beautiful than the vocal rendition. Trevor Key again provided the cover shot, an alternate view of the objects pictured on the 'Thieves Like Us' sleeve, now radiating evil. The 12" was released only through Factory Benelux, much to the chagrin of English fans. Tony Wilson explained, "What we were doing was we had this secondary company, Factory Benelux, in Belgium. We didn't really have the energy to put out a (New Order) album and two or three singles a year, so we decided, 'These spare tracks, why don't they go out through a separate company in Europe and be imported again as interesting imports?' So some stuff would come out in Belgium, that would be different from the stuff in England. It just seemed a groovy thing to do." But the import prices for the single, not to mention the menacing tone of 'Murder', kept it from becoming a hit in Great Britain.

After touring Spain and Germany, New Order spent the late summer on vacation, some band-members' trips more successful than others. Barney, his wife Sue, and son James withdrew to Barbados, and it rained the whole time they were there. Stephen, Gillian, and Kim Gilbert tried to get to Miami, but stayed in New York with Stanton Miranda, recording the pop song 'Wheels Over Indian Trails', named after a graffiti mural welcoming Long Islanders to the former Iroquois territory of Manhattan. The time New Order spent apart made them treasure their friendship. When they all reunited for a tour in August, they felt relaxed and were happy to see each other again.

The tour, half-promoted by Final Solution, stopped at out-of-the-way English villages usually ignored by rock bands. New Order wished to take

in new sights to keep their concerts fresh and interesting, and this tour of the unknown excited them all. Kicking things off at the Mayfair Suite in Sunderland on August 15, 1984, they would drive to every venue in the early afternoon, play onstage, then pack up their gear and drive back to Manchester, repeating the process every day. They hoped the commuting would keep them grounded at home, rather than get them lost in a blinding whirlpool of hotel rooms. Along the way they tested new songs, including the autobiographical 'Sooner Than You Think', the religious 'Sunrise', and a disco song with an already epic arrangement that began as an instrumental, later embellished by Barney's improvised lyrics and eventually titled 'The Perfect Kiss'. One of Barney's ad-libs during 'Hurt' offended the audience at the club Golddiggers in Chippenham. He sang, "I can give you a big piece of my dick... I'll poke you with my prick." Somebody tossed a sneaker at the singer, who picked it up and said, "Will the, uhm, person who threw the shoe up, if he wants it back, come backstage afterwards? And *I'll* give it to him." A gig at the Cornwall Coliseum in St. Austell finished the tour, and New Order studied tapes of the songs they'd débuted for inclusion on a new LP.

In America, most record companies had given up hope of ever signing New Order, viewing the group's demands for creative control as obstinacy. California talent scout Tom Atencio, however, was confident he could work out a deal with the band. He said, "I was working as an Artists and Repertoire man for Quincy Jones' Qwest label. I didn't know exactly how to bring any lustre to Qwest; it had about half a dozen R & B acts, but no modern ones. New Order was one of my favourite bands, and I felt they hadn't signed to any company because they hadn't met the right personality. I didn't know them, but I got Rob Gretton's number and called him up."

Tony Wilson continued the story from there: "What led to the deal with Qwest was New Order never doing a deal in America, always getting near to it, first getting near to it with Geffen, then getting near to it with somebody else. And basically the Los Angeles music industry came to the conclusion that New Order were fucking weird bastards that were never going to sign with anybody, that they were arrogant cunts. They fucking gave up. And Tom Atencio, who had loved New Order from afar, had realised every single fucking person in the music industry was trying to sign them and didn't even bother to go see them. And then three months later he heard that they'd signed to nobody and he thought, 'Oh, that's very (odd)'. A month later he heard that his friend Quincy Jones had just done this deal with (Warner Brothers Records executive) Mo Ostin to do his own label called Qwest, at which point Atencio rings up Warner Brothers and says, 'Listen, do you still want New Order?' And they go, 'Of course we want New Order, but this is ridiculous, no one is going to get New Order, they're not going to sign to anybody.' And Tom said, 'If I can get them to sign to Warner Brothers or a Warner Brothers subsidiary, do I become a key man? Do I come on board? Do I get points?' And they said, 'Of course you do.' So Atencio rang up Quincy and then made a phone call to England.

"And I got a phone call from Rob Gretton saying, 'Ah, a guy just rang me from Quincy Jones' office saying, 'Do you want to be on Quincy Jones' label? It's distributed by Warner Brothers.' And I'm going, 'Wow! Wow! Yeah!' And basically Tom just thought, 'These fucking arrogant English bastards, all I've got to do is ring them up and say, hi, I'm calling for Quincy Jones, would you like to be on our label, and these fuckers will fall for it.' And of course we did. We fell for it hook, line, and sinker, 'What a great idea, what a fabulous thing'."

"They invited me over to see a miners' benefit," Atencio said, "and I flew over, had breakfast with them. I think they were struck with the idea of working with a respected musician."

of Jones' calibre thought their records ranked alongside his own. More importantly, Qwest respected the band's wishes for autonomy. Negotiations began in the fall of '84 for Factory to license New Order's music to Qwest, who would pay for the records upon receipt and make no artistic limitations. "It took me a couple more months and another trip (in February of 1985) to get them committed," Atencio said, but the band agreed to start the deal with its forthcoming album, provisionally titled *Love Vigilantes*, and single, 'The Perfect Kiss'. "(The deal) has worked out great," Wilson said, "because within about a year Qwest had half ceased to exist, and was no longer a really strong record company, it was just an identity. And as such, it works fine. We're very happy with Warner Brothers, and the Qwest thing is fine, but as I say it was very much a red herring, really. It's not quite as significant (of change within the music business) as we think it is."

The album marked New Order's first attempts at social criticism, which unlike Joy Division's work, dealt with issues on a human rather than ideological level. *Love Vigilantes* began with the title track, an unforgettable tale of a soldier consumed with homesickness. He finally goes on leave to visit his family, yet when he enters his house, he discovers his wife crying on the floor, clutching a telegram that said her husband, "was a great, brave man but (is) dead." Had the telegram been sent in error, or was the narrator this man's ghost? 'Love Vigilantes' was a simple character study but incredibly evocative. Having mastered impressionistic lyrics, Barney now felt confident enough to tackle storytelling. He handled the job with ease.

'The Perfect Kiss' was about a man making love with a friend who later dies of AIDS. The gay community had supported New Order's disco songs, and the band no doubt knew at least somebody who was infected or had died. New Order felt moved to remind its audience about the importance of protected sex. The narrator concluded, "Now I know the perfect kiss is the kiss of death." This all-important verse, the one which defined "the perfect kiss", had to be cut to fit the lengthy song onto the album. In its unedited form, 'The Perfect Kiss' grew steadily more complex, Hooky playing bass and drums, Barney handling guitar and percussion, Gillian and Steve playing keyboards. At one interlude, Steve created a chorus of synthesized frog sounds – hundreds of princes waiting to be kissed, any one of whom might be HIV-positive. The cut finally crashed to a conclusion with a squeal, but the arrangement never flew out of control. All of the bandmembers were deservedly proud of the parable they had written.

'This Time Of Night' began with a voice, perhaps Rob Gretton's, saying, "I'm one of the few people who lives what's called the low life." The band eventually re-titled the album *Low Life* because they liked the phrase so much. Hooky got to bang away at his electronic drums again, but his bass was noticeably absent or understated at best. He sang with Barney on the finale, "Whatever you may do to me, don't ever take my dignity."

Loss of dignity and faith energised 'Sunrise', an angry rocker that recalled 'O My God' by The Police. Barney's lyrics were about – and addressed to – 'The Lord above', who wouldn't answer. "I tried so hard last night, you would not talk to me," he accused after a sleepless night of prayer. At dawn, 'God' responded, barely audible above the furiously-played coda, "Whatever I have done for you I did for myself for free." The sentiment recalled Joy Division, but the delivery was completely New Order.

'Elegia', an instrumental lullaby, became widely accepted as New Order's requiem for Ian Curtis. The music, especially the funereal synthesized organ, expressed a spectrum of emotions: joy, grief, anger,

forgiveness, words weren't necessary. The lack of vocals also provided time to reflect upon the losses of life and innocence depicted on the first half of the album. 'Sooner Than You Think' picked up the tempo and told of life after the death of a loved one, specifically life in a rock and roll band. Barney sang about greeting an audience, backstage parties, bruised egos and the habit of flattering hosts. "Your country is a wonderful place," he said, "pales my England into disgrace. To buy a drink there is so much more reasonable. I think I'll go there when it gets seasonable." The high-tech 'Sub-Culture' evoked other lifestyles, especially homosexual and sadomasochistic ones. Barney played percussion on an empty glass bottle, and Hooky's bass, normally so important, took a backseat to Gillian's keyboards.

Steve's drums pounded on 'Face-Up', a giddy, horny jig with a singalong chorus of, "Oh, how I cannot bear the thought of you." To quote from 'Thieves Like Us', love, which inspired all of the songs on *Low Life* – love of home and country, love of spouse, love of God, love of friends and acquaintances, love of wild, magnificent sex – had been revealed as, "the cure for every evil." New Order had discovered the secret of happy living which Joy Division overlooked.

New Order spent seven weeks in the spring of 1985 playing a concert tour of the Far East. During April, the band taped a suite-like disco song about a hit-and-run drunk driving accident called 'State Of The Nation', "which", according to Rob Gretton, "was quite strange. We recorded it for, like, a week or so, and the engineers that recorded it in the night had been working during the day as well. They never slept, except for maybe two or three hours at a time, and they were pretty tired. Japan was pretty weird." New Order's May 2 gig at Tokyo's Koseinenkinkainen Hall, as well as The Durutti Column's show there the week before, were filmed in a joint venture between Factory and Nippon Columbia, the licensees of New Order records in Japan. Both shoots were directed by Tony Wilson. He said, "That was just a piece of shit, that was Nippon Columbia saying they wanted to do a couple of pop-in concerts, could I please come in and do these two videos? The Durutti Column video was much better; I'd much rather be remembered for that. The Durutti Column one I was able to do myself with two 35mm cameras but cheap, but for New Order they insisted on spending a lot of money and putting in the whole fucking TV crew and I couldn't fucking stop them because they're such boring bastards, the Japanese. So it's a very boring video." However, when it was finally released, the video had earned a very unboring title: 'Pumped Full Of Drugs'!

The band travelled to Hong Kong, then Australia, and while they never made it to the beach this time around, Barney, now going by the surname Sumner, did manage to have an (mis-)adventure all his own. In Sydney, after a night of dancing and too much drinking, he came to rest inside a garbage can, feasting on a bowl of fruit salad. At six in the morning, a passer-by handed him a cucumber out of her grocery bag for him to add to his meal. When he sobered up, he still had the uneaten cucumber in his possession, so he decided to keep it as a souvenir and packed it in his suitcase. Customs officials later confiscated the vegetable, either because of quarantine laws or out of concern that Barney was going to do something perverse with it.

New Order's third LP, *Low Life*, came packaged in a greasepaper sheath which listed the band, album, and song names. For once, the record even featured photographs of New Order on the cover! Trevor Key took the four portraits, all distorted in the developing lab for artistic effect. The design of the LP and compact discs were generally the same in every country, but Factory issued the British cassette in a unique box set which

Tony Wilson defended the band's stubbornness. "They didn't mind the Demme video," he said. "Jonathan was filming them playing their instruments, which they don't mind. That's fine: 'We do this, as long as we're filmed playing live, we don't mind. You can film us. We have no problems with that.' It's just, 'If you want me to do anything else, if you want to stand there and take a photograph of me, why? My job is not standing, having my photograph taken, my job is playing a guitar and singing. That's my job, I don't stand there. I'm not a male model.' I think that's their attitude, 'I'm not a model, I'm not an actor, if I wanted to be a model or an actor I'd have got into that. I'm just a fucking musician, leave me alone.' That's their attitude. I applaud it.

"What compromise means, in the end, is doing something that you don't want to do. That's a compromise, right? So basically, they don't compromise. They don't do something they don't want to do. If you had said to them, 'To keep the Hacienda going, you've got to sell out and compromise,' they would have closed the Hacienda down. And so would I have done it. If the Hacienda was forcing them to the point of view where (New Order) were being forced to compromise to make money, where money was taking any precedence...

"No, you can't say that to them, nor would you, nor would you say that to myself. It's unthinkable." New Order's integrity was beyond reproach. On the other hand, this integrity meant the band had to accept that not all of their dreams of wealth and luxury would come easily. As Tony Wilson said, dealing with the musicians meant having conversations like, "'Barney! Barney! Do-you-want-a-yacht?' 'Yeah.' 'Do you want to play on *Top Of The Pops*?' 'Nah.' And you say, 'Barney, don't you realise if you're gonna have a yacht, you've gotta do these things?' 'Yeah? So wot.' Barney would like a yacht, but in no way does that mean Barney will do any of the things you have to do to get a yacht. That is the weird and wonderful thing."

The video for 'The Perfect Kiss' was a nine-minute mini-movie, and to get it broadcast on MTV, which didn't want any lengthy videos taking up its airtime (besides 'Thriller'), Michael Shamberg attempted to edit it down to half of its original length. "I tried to do it in LA," he said, "and the band hadn't approved it, I wasn't happy with it, and (somehow) it got out there. It wasn't used too much, but you should see the long version, that's the only real version." The full-length video was used as a short before many films, including Demme's 'Stop Making Sense', 'The Coca-Cola Kid', and 'Insignificance'.

In June, Qwest released its own American pressing of *Power, Corruption and Lies*, with the cassette and CD versions adding 'Blue Monday' and 'The Beach', which the label issued as a 12" single as well. Rob Gretton had felt the new printings were needed, "Just to get (the records) major distribution," as they had previously been available only as expensive British imports. Two months later, as 'The Perfect Kiss' entered the Top Five of the United States' dance charts, New Order launched a three-week North American tour, which extended from coast to coast and attracted thousands of fans.

The group returned to England in September, affording Peter Hook the opportunity to be with his girlfriend Iris and their baby daughter, Heather. Heather had been born shortly before the Far East tour, which meant Hooky had missed half of her life! The whole band spent time with their family and friends, gearing up for some busy months ahead.

Early October was spent recording a new version of 'State Of The Nation' entitled 'Shame Of The Nation' and a disco epic in the same vein entitled 'Shellshock' with producer John Robie. Robie met New Order through Arthur Baker and Michael Shamberg, and had a reputation of being a hotshot craftsman of dance songs. During the sessions, Robie suggested that the band transpose its music into a different key, one better suited to Barney's range. The notes themselves would stay the same, but Barney would have an easier time of singing to them, without straining or having his voice crack (two constant problems he'd learned to live with). Peter Hook immediately got upset, and told Robie not to try and change the band's method of playing. He wasn't doing anything of the sort, Robie explained, only trying to help out. New Order took his advice, and the sessions found Barney performing with more vocal control than ever before.

New Order toured Great Britain in October and November, as Factory released two remixes of the *Low Life* track 'Sub-Culture' on a 12" single with a plain black sleeve. It stalled at No 63 – the worst of any New Order single before or since – but the band probably weren't bothered with its chart showing. They were already divided in opinion over the remixes which Robie had done in America, and even if the songs didn't sell well, they garnered lots of airplay in dance clubs, the environment for which the tracks were best suited.

In January 1986, New Order participated in With Love From Manchester, a benefit gig held in Liverpool to raise money for the city's

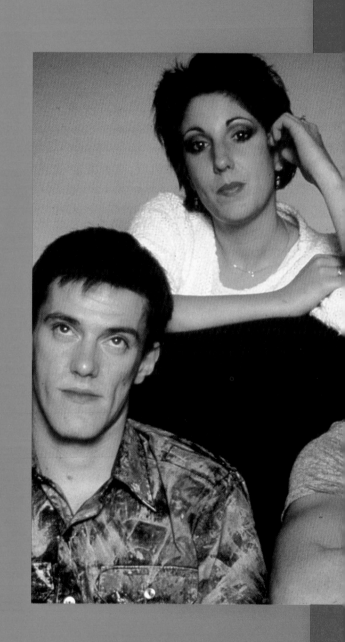

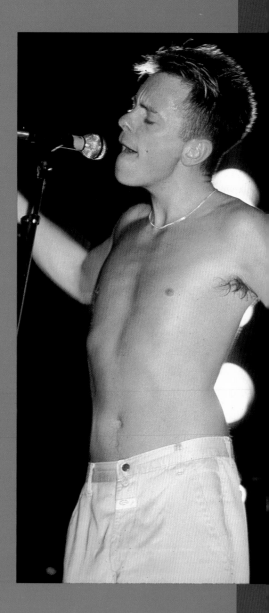

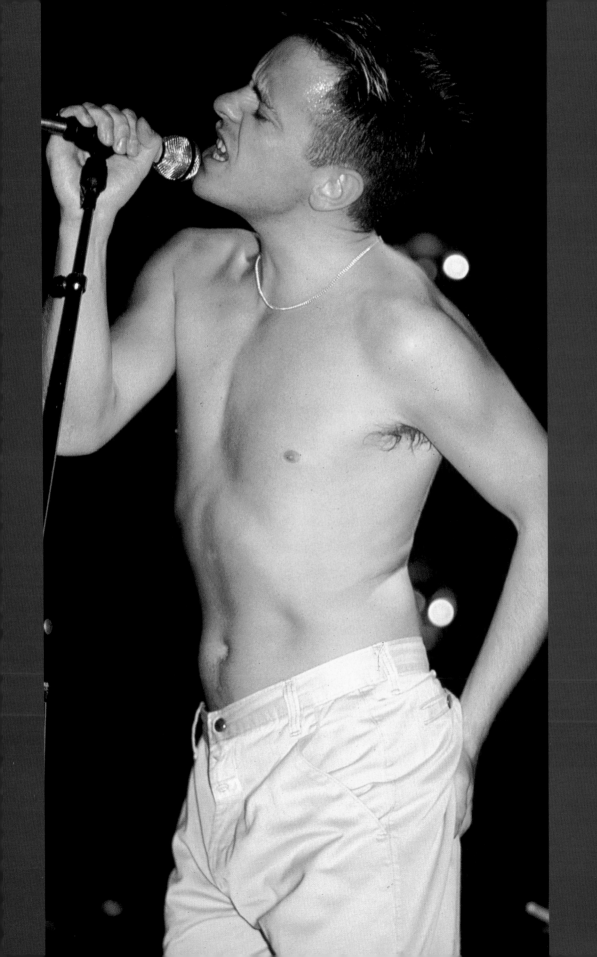

Right and below:
At The Hacienda.

local council, who were being sued by the British government for not cutting jobs and services. New Order opened the gig, introduced by ABC's Martin Fry, and closed their set with 'Love Will Tear Us Apart': a surprise for everyone in attendance which reaffirmed their strength following Ian's death.

Barney spoke backstage with Johnny Marr of The Smiths, who were also playing on the bill. Barney had written a song for New Order called 'Gangster' which did not suit the group's style of music, but might work if it featured Marr's jangly guitar. He began to think about collaborating with this fellow Mancunian who'd become a hero to many of his generation.

New Order returned to America shortly thereafter to work some more with Robie on 'Shame Of The Nation', and also attend the gala première of *Pretty In Pink*, a new John Hughes movie which used 'Thieves Like Us', 'Elegia' and 'Shellshock' in its soundtrack, the last of which had been specially written for this movie. All of the bands involved were invited to the party and screening at Grauman's Chinese Theater in Los Angeles, and like all Hollywood events, this one attracted dozens of reporters and cameramen. The photographers wanted to take a picture of every celebrity, but didn't know all of the musical acts on sight. So as Rob Gretton, Barney Sumner, Gillian Gilbert, Stephen Morris and Peter Hook walked up to the theatre's entrance, they were asked by the press where New Order was. The band pointed to some roadies standing near the door. The photographers believed them and dashed off, as the real New Order laughed all the way inside.

A & M Records released the *Pretty In Pink* soundtrack LP in February '86, as well as a 12" of 'Shellshock' b/w 'Thieves Like Us (Instrumental)'. Tom Atencio thought it was brave of Qwest to permit a rival company to release the songs, especially when 'Shellshock' sounded like hit material. He said, "It was an interesting move, lending out a new track. It was an entirely new construction. It was kind and visionary on the part of Warner Brothers, and was a very successful track." It certainly was, both in America, where the film and album gave lots of people their first exposure to New Order, and in England, where the song, b/w the chaotic remix 'Shellcock', climbed to No 28 on the singles chart.

The summer was spent recording a new LP. The first track New Order completed was a goofy, irrepressible tribute to Lou Reed's 'Walk On The Wild Side' entitled 'Every Little Counts': "Every little counts when I am with you. I think you are a pig, you should be in a zoo." Barney couldn't sing these lyrics without cracking up, and the band decided to leave his in-the-studio chuckling on the final version, which Tom Atencio had to endure presenting to Warner Brothers executives as an indication of what the new album would sound like. One can only imagine what the reaction was like in the boardroom.

The rest of the album followed in the style of *Low Life*, some tracks heavy on guitars, others centred around keyboards and syndrums. The introductory 'Paradise' yearned for someone or something to instil a sense of belonging, either a woman or simply a home. 'Weirdo' raced along, "just like the ocean and the sea, just like the blood that runs in me", while guitars and drums sprinted to the finishing line. The wistful 'As It Is When It Was' had been debuted on 'Pumped Full Of Drugs'; here its ending piled sad ideas one atop the other, including , "In a world where I've forgotten you, I find myself forgotten too." The fast-tempoed 'Broken Promise' and 'Way Of Life' were directed towards estranged lovers, the former accusing that, "the things that mean so much to me don't mean that much to you," the latter asking, "Who do you think you're talking to? When I look at you I know you're lying." The feelings of empathy expressed on the last album had been worn away; honeymoons were over, and now mates had to speak

plainly about the things which bothered them. Side one ended on a hopeful note, Peter Hook grinding away at his bass and then gently picking out a tender melody.

Side two opened with the Technicolor burst of 'Bizarre Love Triangle', Gillian's keyboards and Hook's bass fighting to dominate the song with some of the loveliest chord progressions they'd ever written. New Order smartly followed this carefree extravaganza with two morality tales about the results of irresponsibility. 'All Day Long' was about child abduction and molestation, a subject which had terrified Barney since the birth of his son, James. The words honestly described parents' contradictory feelings of love and anger at their children, saying, "He'd drive me crazy, he'd drive me wild. I used to scream and shout all day long." After the narrator's son is kidnapped, he screams and shouts because he feels powerless to save his boy. 'Angel Dust', told from the drug's point of view, offered an evil counterpoint to this cautionary tale. "You never knew," Barney sang, "with open arms I came to you. Judging me so safe to be with, mistakes you made that you can't live with." Guitars howled and pianos chimed in minor keys. This was their most horrific work since 'Murder'. Both 'All Day Long' and 'Angel Dust' enjoyed lengthy, moody arrangements, which set up the

finale 'Every Little Counts' as even more of an oddball than it really was. New Order created a distorted ending for it, obviously based on 'A Day In The Life' by The Beatles. At the moment when 'Every Little Counts' seemed to absolutely lose its way, the sound of a phonograph needle skipping off the LP's grooves freed the band from having to recover the song structure. Stephen Morris later wished they had recorded a different ending for each recording format: the sound of a needle skipping for the album, the sound of magnetic tape getting eaten for the cassette, and the sound of a CD sticking for the compact disc. New Order broke away from the studio in June to play at an anti-Apartheid concert in Sheffield, and performed again in July, for the tenth anniversary celebration of the birth of Manchester's music community, the Festival of the Tenth Summer.

The "official" birth took place with the formation of The Buzzcocks in 1976, but the scene had flowered just as much as a result of The Sex Pistols' gig at the Free Trade Hall so many years ago, when Barney, Hooky, Ian Curtis and Terry Mason all began to think about forming bands. The festival began with art exhibitions by Peter Saville and designer Malcolm Garrett, and ended at the Greater Manchester Exhibition Hall with performances by A Certain Ratio, The Negatives, The Worst, The Virgin Prunes (who were, interestingly enough, Irish), John Cooper-Clarke, OMD, Bill Grundy, The Fall, Sandy Shaw, Pete Shelly, Steve Diggle, and New Order. The band started its set with 'Elegia', remembering that Ian Curtis deserved to be at this event just as much as anybody, and ended it with 'Ceremony', the legacy that Joy Division bequeathed to the world. In between, New Order whipped the crowd of eight thousand neighbours into a frenzy, repaying their love from the stage, and the group later declared that this gig had been one of the highlights of their year.

After postponing its release so as not to interfere with the success of 'Shellshock', Factory released the single 'State Of The Nation' backed with the John Robie/New Order collaboration 'Shame Of The Nation' in August. A second New Order disc followed, an EP of the band's 1982 John Peel session, issued by Peel's own label, Strange Fruit Records. Four years from their date of recording, time had not improved the songs at all. They were an interesting history lesson, but not very entertaining. Joy Division's two Peel Sessions, and New Order's first were subsequently released, but only the Joy Division material sparkled. To hear the songs without Martin Hannett's embellishing was fascinating.

Factory also released 'Freaky Dancing' backed with 'The Egg' by Happy Mondays as a 7" and 12" single. Barney Sumner had produced the tracks, striking up a friendship with the rag-tag Mondays in the process. Their band, like The Stiff Kittens, had been formed on a friendship. He liked the musicians a lot.

New Order spent five days in September writing and recording music for *Salvation!*, a movie satirising American televangelists which starred Exene Cervenka of the rock band X. Michael Shamberg co-produced the film, and said New Order, "had watched some scenes, then Beth B., the director, went over and worked with the band. They worked really fast and they all really enjoyed it, and although it was a low-budget situation, that even added to the fun. It was like they were a band again, and they had to write something really quick, and record it really quick – quick and rough. I think Hooky liked it the most, 'cause he likes that way of working. He likes that real 'band' element, the acoustic element. I think he was really pleased that we didn't take his bass out." New Order provided 'Salvation Theme', vocal and instrumental versions of 'Let's Go' (Shamberg chose the latter for the film), 'Sputnik', 'Skullcrusher', and a collaboration with Arthur Baker, 'Touched By The Hand Of God.' 'Touched...' vividly captured the sexual/spiritual relationship between TV preachers and their audiences. That New Order could bang out such an evocative track at such short notice was a testament to their ability to work as a unit. It was fitting that they named their new album *Brotherhood*.

Barney and Tony Wilson hated *Brotherhood*'s production, Wilson going so far as to call it, "a fucking shitty album". "It sounds terrible," Wilson said. "It sounds absolutely terrible. I mean, they're a great group, so their songs are going to be better than anybody else's, but I found the sound quality very unattractive. I suggested remixing it, but everyone goes, 'Oh no, fuck off.' No, *Brotherhood* is generally accepted now by certain people, including me. Someone was beside me last night, saying, 'No! No! No! It was great, man, it was fucking great, it had that fucking great track on it, blah blah blah, and that track, blah blah blah,' and I said, 'You're talking about *Low Life*.' And he went, 'Tsk, so I am. Oh my God, yeah, *Brotherhood*.' 'Exactly,' I said, ' you haven't played it in three years.' Proves my point. *Brotherhood* was a disaster.

"Basically, it's the year of New Order and (sound engineer) Michael Johnson producing themselves. I suppose I became more and more against that. But of course, if you like *Brotherhood*, God bless you."

Tony Wilson.

New Order ✝ Joy Division

The release of *Brotherhood* on September 30, 1986 was marked at White Columns, the art gallery and "alternative space" downstairs from Of Factory New York. Peter Saville attended the listening party – although few people seemed to recognise the record on the turntable as New Order's – and he admitted to liking the band members as friends, but not necessarily as musicians. Saville's "metallic" sleeve design for *Brotherhood* was echoed in 'Compact', a painted steel sculpture he'd designed after a piece of a cardboard box, then on display at White Columns as a part of the LP promotion. New Order remained in England, giving interviews to the press and playing a handful of concerts, then flew to America in late October for their largest tour to date.

The tour began on October 29 at Phoenix, Arizona's Mesa Amphitheater, followed by a week in California, then dates in Utah, Colorado, Texas, Pennsylvania, New York, Massachusetts, Washington DC, and Georgia, coming to a sunny conclusion in Miami, Florida on December 15. The group did two shows in Manhattan. One took place at the Felt Forum, where The Sex Pistols' 'God Save The Queen' was played over the P.A. right before New Order took the stage. The song got the audience pogoing merrily, and the band didn't let them slow down for the rest of the night. Everyone left a sweaty, sticky mess, ticket stubs crumbling inside sopping-wet pants pockets. Hooky sported a fetching t-shirt for Club Maitresse, the nightclub at Falconberg Court hosted by *Skin Two* magazine, a very elegant – and very expensive – periodical dedicated to the S & M lifestyle. Barney took off his top and spent an hour pulling up his oversized grey slacks in time to the music. Stephen bobbed his head and smiled, delighted with the performance. Gillian simply looked bored. The other concert was a hastily-arranged benefit for the family of the late talent scout Ruth Polsky, held at the nightspot 1018. Polsky had booked Joy Division's cancelled gig at Hurrah, as well as New Order's first American tour. The band had hired her to work as road manager for these *Brotherhood* gigs, but she had been killed by a taxicab before the band reached America. New Order, Michael Shamberg, and everyone associated with the group mourned Polsky's death.

The extensive tour could only help the album, as well as its single, 'Bizarre Love Triangle', released in 7" and 12" formats. Factory backed it with a remix, 'Bizarre Dub Triangle', while Qwest used 'Every Little Counts' on the 7"; 'State Of The Nation' and two remixes of the A-side on the 12". Michael Shamberg produced the 'B.L.T.' video, hiring artist Robert Longo to direct it.

"I had known Robert for some time because I used to work in a place in New York called the Kitchen, and he came there to work when I was leaving. We hung out for a while, and then we just didn't see each other. Steve Baker at Warner Brothers called me up and recommended that Longo work on the video, and I thought, 'Well, isn't that odd? Well, let's go see him.' And I thought maybe he was upset with me; I found out later he thought I was upset with him. We got along quite well... He claimed that New Order and Joy Division were very influential on his work. Tony Wilson had sent some cameramen from Granada TV to Italy, and they took a lot of footage. There's the band on different hills, live footage... Those first shots that open the piece, the four head shots, were also done in Italy." Longo's abstract collection of images for 'Bizarre Love Triangle' included flashes of 'Compact' and a spoken word segment of a man and two women dropped right into the middle of the song: a bizarre love triangle! MTV gave the clip some airplay, and the brilliant chorus, "Every time I see you falling, I get down on my knees and pray," inspired people to buy the single – and *Brotherhood* – in volume.

New Order embarked on its second Far East tour in January, 1987, and the band didn't settle down until late February or early March. The time at home allowed them to pursue one of Rob Gretton's ideas, a digitally remastered collection of New Order's non-LP tracks. Work by every artist from Louis Armstrong to The Beatles had come out on compact disc, and he and the band felt it was time for them to join the CD revolution. Tony Wilson saw this as a great opportunity to give 'Temptation' a second chance at being a hit, and he told the group, "Listen, we should have a single off (the collection), why don't we do a modernised version of 'Temptation'? We'll do a real modern version, put the old version on the B-side. That'll be the single to come out of the compilation."

Months passed, and Wilson forgot about 'Temptation'. Producer Stephen Hague and Tom Atencio suggested that New Order write a new song to promote the LP, and Wilson thought, "Fine, okay. That'll be the twelfth single. I can have twelve songs on the album, the Stephen Hague one will be the single off of it." So in May 1987, he was dumbstruck when Rob Gretton told him, "They're going into the studio to re-do 'Temptation'."

"Wuh – well, why?" Wilson asked.

"We were talking about it," Gretton said. "It was your idea."

"I know, but we don't need it now; we're doing this thing with Hague."

New Order believed a collection of their singles ought to feature their favourite arrangements of their hits, and since the band performed 'Temptation' – as well as 'Confusion' – differently in concert than they had been recorded, they felt obliged to re-record them for the album. Wilson listened to the re-makes and argued, "These two things, they're out of place. They don't even prove the songs. In fact, they don't seem as good as the originals." New Order disagreed with him, but as a concession, agreed to include Arthur Baker's instrumental version of 'Confusion' on a second volume of B-sides. "That took me about five minutes to win that one, actually," Wilson said. "As long as there was a bit of Arthur Baker's version, which was the classic version, that was all I was worried about."

The film *Salvation!* had its world première at the Berlin Film Festival on May 31, 1987, roughly the same time as several televangelists were scandalised for raping their followers or claiming God was holding them for ransom to pay for churches made of crystal. The timeliness of the movie's plot couldn't have been better, but Warner Brothers Records feared a soundtrack album might steal attention (and fans' spending money) away from the forthcoming New Order greatest hits package. The *Salvation!* soundtrack was delayed until 1988.

The greatest hits collection, called *Substance*, was preceded by the single 'True Faith' b/w '1963', both co-written by New Order and Stephen Hague. 'True Faith' melded Hooky's bass guitar rock with Gillian's synthe-sizer symphonies into a thunderous tale of a man betrayed by his religious leaders, and the sound generated airplay in clubs and radio stations on both sides of the Atlantic. The B-side, '1963', also became popular, despite its melodramatic lyrics about a jilted boyfriend who visits his ex-lover on her birthday and kills her. For the 12", Madonna's producer Shep Pettibone modified 'True Faith' into 'The Morning Sun Remix', the 'Alternate Faith Dub', and a third re-interpretation, 'The Morning Sun', which appeared on a promo-only 7" single distributed to radio DJs. 'True Faith' went to number four in England and reached the number thirty-two position in the US. After years of being unjustly ignored, New Order had become American radio staples. The college-radio disc jockeys who had grown up with the band in the early part of the decade were remaining loyal to New Order as they landed jobs with commercial stations.

One of the strongest assets supporting 'True Faith' was its eccentric video, directed by French choreographer Phillippe DeCouffle. Michael

New Order + Joy Division

Shamberg explained, "(The clip) was filmed in Paris. The band part was filmed in Glastonbury; it was the only way to get them if they were going to be in the video, because they were going on vacation. We shot them, then went back to Paris. Phillippe worked out a scheme in which to connect a dance routine with the band footage, which appeared on the little screen that a character in the video wore." The clip succeeded as both a promotional tool and as a work of art, going into heavy rotation on music video channels and winning awards from various organisations.

New Order's business affairs – namely the Hacienda – were also going well. Tony Wilson said, "What needed to be done was a person had to become the club. Leadership, whatever else, it's an individual thing. An individual had to run the club, run it tight, and know how to do it like a professional. A man called Paul Mason. He ran, very successfully, a club in Nottingham called Rock City. It had been losing a bit of money, and he turned it around." Mason was now working the same magic for the Hacienda, helping it to clear a profit for the first time in its existence.

New Order booked an American tour to promote *Substance*, and did so with an interesting twist by inviting their friends Echo And The Bunnymen – who also had a greatest hits package out – to co-headline the tour, the headlining spot for every evening being decided with the flip of a coin. The pop group Gene Loves Jezebel was added as the opening act. The package tour of the year began in Minneapolis, Minnesota on August 13, and four days later, *Substance* was released to the world.

In England and America, the double LP featured twelve songs, all key tracks from New Order's singles (including the re-recorded 'Confusion' and 'Temptation'). The two-CD set managed to fit all these hits on one volume, and twelve additional B-sides on another. The Factory cassettes of *Substance* also featured the B-sides, but the Qwest pressing did not, despite pre-release memos to record stores insisting they would. As Tom Atencio said, "Cassettes already outsell vinyl... it was already a double album, and to make the cassettes that way seemed gratuitous." *Substance* had been created for the purpose of releasing New Order's considerable number of non-LP tracks in a CD format, so the band weren't concerned that the B-sides might not appear everywhere on tape. The critics and public both embraced the collection for its scope and majesty. *Substance* entered the UK charts at number three, climbed into the top forty in America, and sold over two million copies worldwide.

New Order and Echo And The Bunnymen toured North America throughout August. Not every venue sold out, but people who attended enjoyed many surprises, including both bands performing 'Sister Ray' together at the Mann Music Center in Philadelphia, and Barney's playful taunts in Manhattan, "I know everybody says it, but we do love New York. The drugs are so cheap here. And plentiful!" A concert at Long Island's outdoor Jones Beach Theater was rescheduled due to rain, but New Order rewarded the crowd's patience with a devastating rendition of 'The Perfect Kiss'. On September 3, they played Toronto's C.N.E. Grandstand, the biggest (14,892 people) and most profitable (gross: $255,166) night of the tour. After hitting Buffalo, Pittsburgh, Denver, Salt Lake City, San Diego, Irvine, Los Angeles, and Phoenix, the tour ended with two nights at Berkeley's Greek Theater, September 18 and 19, 1987.

The trip had been an enjoyable but stressful experience for New Order. A friendly rivalry between the band and the Bunnymen encouraged both groups to perform well, yet media attention and the dehumanising atmosphere of massive arenas made New Order uncomfortable. 'True Faith', *Substance*, the tour and the revitalised Hacienda had boosted the bandmembers' weekly wages from £103.50 to £300 a week, and they all owned company cars, but with the money came pressures and

New Order + Joy Division

NEW
ORDER
—
SUBSTANCE
1987

responsibilities. New Order compensated by taking an interest in the business side of their careers. The media, however, assumed the band would crack under the strain and split up. Robert Gretton said a breakup was never even discussed, but New Order decided to issue a press release directed at the rumour mongers: "Up your bum!" Yet there was no way the band could laugh away the fact that releasing an album no longer held as much excitement for them as it once had. They knew what to expect from recording, mixing, pressing and promoting a record. The North American tour, and the English shows that they played before and after it, were among their biggest gigs ever. New Order found themselves a hair's-breadth away from becoming megastars in North America. They could have sought more fame, but instead they made a conscious decision to avoid mainstream popularity.

Like New Order, the Irish band U2 had built an American cult following for the past seven years, and in 1987, U2 exploded, performing an exhausting world tour, relinquishing most of their free time to give interviews, and losing their privacy to the glare of media scrutiny. New Order considered the rewards U2 had earned in return for their personal lives – two number one singles, a number one album – and were horrified. The payoff didn't seem to warrant the price. New Order were afraid to get any larger, for fear of losing their privacy, their control over the band, and their principles. They pulled back the reins on their careers by refusing to tour and release singles as often as they could have, limiting the number of interviews they would grant (preferring to focus on glossy magazines, according to their talent agency, Triad), and allowing each other to work on solo projects.

This last agreement was the result of years of internal arguments and compromises, all four bandmembers bending over backwards to make each other happy. Barney wanted to release music without conceding to Gillian, Stephen, and Hooky, and his solo project, provisionally known as Sell Your Body, was intended as an all-star band featuring himself and Johnny Marr, his guitarist friend who'd recently quit The Smiths. The duo jammed and rehearsed at weekends, separating when other obligations demanded their time. Peter Hook responded by forming the group Revenge with two of his buddies, guitarist Dave Hicks and a keyboardist named Chris Jones, the engineer at Hooky's personal recording studio, Suite 16. That either man felt he could not express himself properly within New Order was upsetting to the other bandmembers as well as some fans. The four friends divided three ways and grew estranged from each other.

New Order + Joy Division

The Price of Love

New Order returned to England. Besides a live performance of 'True Faith' on *Top Of The Pops* and a concert in England, they spent the end of the year separated. They would not split up, but would rarely again seem as unified as they had once been.

The *Salvation!* soundtrack LP came out in January, 1988. A remixed version of 'Touched By The Hand Of God' was issued by Factory as a single, backed with a dub version on the vinyl record; a remix of the new 'Confusion', and, accidentally, the *Substance* rendition of 'Temptation' on the CD. According to Tony Wilson, the compact disc was supposed to include the original version of 'Temptation', but, "Some moron had actually put the new version on it. So it says, 'Temptation (Old Version)' on it but it's got the new version on it. I gave up."

Michael Shamberg produced the hilarious video for 'Touched By The Hand Of God', a parody of the heavy metal videos New Order had watched on TV while touring America. New Order wanted to expose the stupidity and pretentiousness of metal bands, and as such were willing to dress up in "rock and roll" clothing, put on frightwigs, and lip sync, despite the group's long-maintained refusal to mime in their videos. "That was part of the concept," Shamberg said. "A heavy metal band does do that, so it wasn't really New Order." Despite the fact that Hooky wasn't really acting in the clip – his hair had already grown to his shoulders, he wore leather, and played bass with the instrument dangling near his feet – the rest of the band revelled in their alter egos as rock monsters, and for once, appeared to have a blast in one of their promo films. Warner Brothers records worried about New Order's easy adoption of headbanger traditions, going so far as to not release 'Touched By The Hand Of God' as a single, and by all impressions, suppressing the video. "I think Warner Brothers was concerned and scared that the video might have given people who didn't have an image of the band the wrong impression," Shamberg said. It was rarely shown, despite the fame of its director, Kathyryn Bigelow, and fifth star, *Aliens, Terminator*, and *Near Dark* scenestealer Bill Paxton.

Warner Brothers and Qwest had their eyes on 'Blue Monday 1988', an updated version of the 1983 hit. They felt this, rather than 'Touched By The Hand Of God', should be the follow-up to 'True Faith' and would best represent/promote New Order in America. The band recorded overdubs that production supervisor Quincy Jones could incorporate into the song, but he didn't use the new vocal or drum tracks. The version he created dispelled the original's intensity in favour of a more jubilant, partylike atmosphere. In effect, he created a totally new song.

"I was trying to think of something that was different," Shamberg said of the 'Blue Monday 1988' video, "something fresh. I was interested in doing something with animation, I didn't know what. I looked in a Whitney Biennial Catalog , saw two frames, one was a ball, one was a person, very crudely hand drawn, and said, 'That's it!'" The artist who'd sketched the pictures was film-maker Robert Breer. Shamberg met Breer, asked if he'd do a New Order video, and he said yes. Shamberg also knew William Wegman, a director of short comedies known for his work with his pet dogs Man Ray (by that time deceased) and Fay Ray, both of which were hams before a camera.

Shamberg said, "I felt that if the two of them could get together, Wegman would utilise his trained dog, Fay Ray, and also deal with the band. Breer would be able to work off of Wegman, back and forth, and their humour, I felt, was quite good. They got along, and in the end the editor brought them together, and they were quite happy with the video."

New Order were filmed in Los Angeles while in town as the halftime entertainment at a fashion show attended by the Duke and Duchess of York. Wegman pelted the band with rubber balls, filmed them playing with flip-books, and balanced Fay on a series of delicate and precarious props. The clip revealed the sillier sides of the musicians' personalities just as 'Touched By The Hand Of God' had, but in this film, there was no acting. 'Blue Monday 1988' dispelled New Order's reputation as moody shoegazers for all time, showing they were easy to laughter and disarmingly "normal", despite their success. It helped their public images tremendously.

Factory released short and extended length versions of 'Blue Monday 1988' and its dub version, 'Beach Buggy', on 7", 12", and CD singles. Qwest coupled 'Blue Monday 1988' with 'Touched By The Hand Of God' on the 7", plus extended versions and new dub versions on the 12".

In America, the remixes ascended the Top Ten of *Billboard*'s 12" sales chart, but the 7" barely registered. Rob Gretton said, "It was quite a big hit in England; that's the place we're mainly concerned with. Anything that happens in America is a bonus, really. The American chart's quite weird. 'True Faith' got to number thirty-two on the chart, 'Blue Monday '88' got nowhere, but we actually sold a lot more 'Blue Monday 1988' records. In America, the charts are based on sales and radio. 'Blue Monday 1988' never got as much airplay as 'True Faith', and as such, didn't do as well."

In addition, Warner Brothers neglected the B-side, 'Touched By The Hand Of God', which may have otherwise helped the single. 'Blue Monday 1988' went Top Twenty in West Germany, Top Ten on the Pan-European chart, and to number four in Britain.

A final opportunity to make 'Blue Monday 1988' a smash came from the Sunkist soda pop company. The firm asked New Order to re-record the lyrics for a TV commercial, and at one point, Barney actually entered a studio to record the altered lyrics:

"Sunkist is the one..."

Then he came to his senses and the deal was called off.

A new remix of 'True Faith' appeared on the soundtrack of the Michael J. Fox drama 'Bright Lights, Big City', which the optimistic staff at Warner Brothers nicknamed, *Bright Lights, Big Singles*. Factory had even higher hopes – and grander plans – for a CD release of Joy Division's non-LP tracks, to be called *Substance* just like the New Order collection. Rumours shot through the New Order and Joy Division fan community that one of the many unreleased takes of 'Love Will Tear Us Apart' would come out as a

New Order ┼ **Joy Division**

Flesh Night at Manchester's Hacienda.

single, but it was the classic rendition of 'Atmosphere' that Factory released in June, 1988. The vinyl single added 'Dead Souls', while the CD featured 'Atmosphere', 'The Only Mistake', 'Sound of Music', and a live version of 'Transmission' recorded at the original Factory Club. The 'Atmosphere' video, directed by one of New Order and Joy Division's favourite photographers, Anton Corbijn, evoked strong reactions from everyone who saw it. Corbijn had visited Peter Saville Associates, the studio which Saville and partner Brett Wickens worked in, and saw the then-unreleased sleeve designs for 'Atmosphere' and Joy Division's *Substance*. The sculptures 'Plus En Min' and 'Energie Piek-Ijs' by artist Jan Van Munster were intrinsic to the designs, and Corbijn appropriated their images for the video, without Saville's knowledge or permission. Corbijn also referred to the cover of *Licht Und Blindheit* by casting children – or midgets – in the roles of hooded monks, most of them carrying giant Corbijn portraits of Ian Curtis along a Spanish coastline. The references to the death cult which had formed since Ian's suicide were blatant, a bit awe-inspiring, and often funny.

Michael Shamberg did not work on the video, but he made some interesting observations. "When it first came out," he said, "the sleeve for 'Atmosphere' was very 1980, and there was a certain style: the 'gloom and doom.' Now that they're re-releasing it, there's no reason it should be like that anymore. The image of the song should be 'now'. That's why the sleeve and the work Peter Saville was doing in 1988 was much more vibrant. The video should not be heard in the context of when 'Atmosphere' was first released, but as it is heard now. Therefore, I think it should have been filmed in 35mm colour, not black and white Super-8, which was very beautiful, but to me, just totally wrong. Tony Wilson put it together, and his reasoning was correct in that Anton Corbijn (should direct because he) had done the photos of the band, but I didn't like it. I think Hooky and Barney liked it because it was different. Steve and Gillian weren't as excited, nor was Rob Gretton."

Gretton explained his position by saying, "The video was a bit reverential, really, and a bit corny. And it seemed to concentrate on Ian, where Ian wasn't particularly the focal point of Joy Division, just as Barney isn't particularly the focal point of New Order. But it tended to concentrate on glorifying Ian more than anything else. I didn't have anything to do with it because I was on a holiday when it was done. I quite like the way it was shot, the style, I think it's quite a well-made video if you don't mind the concept behind it."

Tony Wilson replied, "He likes the way the Super-8 was used to shoot the images and absolutely abhorred the video and blamed me. I thought it was fine. I wanted to sell a dead rock star. I had no qualms about it; the guy is a myth. Basically, whatever video we did with Joy Division, we were going to feel very strange about. It was going to be a strange event. That was my feeling. And therefore it was my decision that by using Anton, a videomaker who shot the original stills, *the* photographer who was there with the group, by using him to make the video and letting him do what he wanted, there would be integrity. That was my only feeling; I was very concerned about it. I was very pleased with the end result."

Joy Division's *Substance* CD followed a few weeks after 'Atmosphere'. It collected the tracks from *An Ideal For Living, A Factory Sample, Earcom 2: Contradiction*, and *Licht Und Blindheit*, plus 'Transmission', 'Novelty', 'She's Lost Control', 'Komakino', 'Incubation', 'These Days' and 'Love Will Tear Us Apart'. The compact disc featured all seventeen tracks, while the LP and cassette only included a sampling of ten A-sides. Unlike *Still*, this collection was greeted without hostility. Just about everyone had recovered

New Order + Joy Division

from Ian's death, and the members of New Order looked back at the era of 1977-1980 as a very romantic and innocent time of their lives. They spoke about Joy Division more freely than they ever had before. They had come to terms with their past, and were ready to accept the future.

New Order's future lay with acid house, the drug-fuelled style of music erupting out of the UK. The band had chosen to record its forthcoming album on the island of Ibiza, itself the birthplace and spawning ground of the movement, which was carried back to England by summer tourists. As Tony Wilson explained, "Acid House, first of all, has nothing to do with acid, or only very, very, very, very marginally. It has everything to do with ecstasy. Until the spring of 1988, Acid House was big only in Derby, Nottingham, and Manchester (at the Hacienda). It wasn't big in London. In the spring, acid house began to come through, which to us, in England, seemed to be like American house music, only even more instrumental this time, with maybe a little bit of Indian and Middle Eastern sounds added.

"Now what acid house is, the general meaning, is a scene where people go wild and take ecstasy and dance all night like crazy with their arms way up in the air. And it's largely to acid house music, but it's also to house music, it's also to Balearic, it's also to electro, and also to punk occasionally. So there's both a specific meaning of the word, but the general meaning is a wild dance scene which is sweeping the country and involves the drug E. It's the most exciting it's been in Britain since '76 by a long way. "This culture has come from the yobbos, the yobs, you know, people who go to football matches and fight. And these same people, when they go on holiday, they go to Ibiza, which is this wild Spanish island in the Mediterranean. They fly there, it's about eighty dollars return flight, with five nights in this concrete jungle kind of place. They have a great time, they just fuck and they drink. And suddenly they'd started going to these massive, massive open-air discos, take three, four, five thousand people, an incredible discotheque. And this Balearic Beat thing started happening.

"This scene was taking off amongst those people in Ibiza, and it was taking off back in England. And that's why it's such a vibrant scene, because it didn't come out of *NME*, didn't come out of the media, didn't come out of *The Face* or *i-D* magazine, it came out of the football terraces, and the kids in England themselves, it came from what they were doing on holiday in Ibiza, which is, as I say, a great working-class holiday island.

"New Order were over there (as the scene became popular), they were already into the scene from being part of the initial movement in England. Their club being the home of it, they'd go out and have a good time. But as Rob said, the thing about the whole ecstasy business, the whole E business, is that his group are, together with The Pet Shop Boys, the main dance-music group in Europe, and New Order never used to fucking dance. They haven't danced for ten years, and now they dance again. So, yes, they're a part of it."

The working titles of the band's new songs reflected their renewed interest in dance music: 'Balearic Beat', 'The Balearic One', 'The Acoustic One', 'The Funky One', 'The Disco One', 'The Housey One', 'The Happy One', 'Eight Track Number One' and 'Eight Track Number Two'. As with many New Order compositions, the titles the band eventually chose to use for these songs had little or nothing to do with the songs themselves. Tony Wilson approached the band during the latter stages of recording at Peter Gabriel's Real World studios in Box, England to ask which track they had chosen as the album's first single.

"You've got to decide the single now, 'cause Factory is going to do the sleeve," Wilson said.

"Why do we have to decide the single if you're going to do the sleeve?" they asked.

"Well, 'cause you've got to get the fucking sleeve done with the title on it!"

The band thought for a moment. "So we'll decide what the title is," they said.

"That'll do."

"Come back in two or three weeks and we'll tell you what the title is."

"That's cool."

New Order decided to call the single 'Fine Time', but still hadn't decided which of the many songs they'd recorded would be named 'Fine Time'. After the sleeve had been laid out, they decided 'Fine Time' would be the new name for 'Balearic Beat'. "That's typical of them," Wilson laughed, "absolutely typical. Their song titles never have any relationship to the songs whatsoever."

'Fine Time (7" Edit)', backed with 'Don't Do It', came out on November 21, 1988, much later than had been planned due to a shortage of available vinyl pressing plants in Europe. Its acid house style made it an immediate club favourite, and in an electronically-distorted vocal line, Barney sang a lyric which gave the LP its title: "You've got style. You've got class. But most of all – you've got love technique."

Rob Gretton called *Technique*, "The first LP we've recorded that is as good as Joy Division. All the tracks are really good. I'm really proud."

Tony Wilson said, "God knows what this album *Technique* is. The great thing that happened was Alan Meyerson, the producer-engineer, was able to clothe both the dance tracks and the rock tracks in the same sound/ambient world. Because basically with New Order you can say, 'Hey, let's do a black dance album.' 'Nah, let's do a rock album.' You can go either way.

"A real album should somehow glue together, should have some kind of feel and go from beginning to end as a piece of work. *Technique* is held together by being Barney's blood on the tracks. It's held together by being produced by a man with one particular vision of sound. It's more at peace than ever before. I think it's their first album to date."

A 'Silk Mix' and 'Messed Around Mix' of 'Fine Time' also became available on a 12" and CD, while the instrumental version 'Fine Line' appeared on cassette and vinyl maxi-singles in Canada. The promotional video reflected the acid house influence on the song. Director Richard

Heslop's clip – which did not feature the band – developed from the lyric, "You're much too young to mess around with me," casting a boy and his dog as E-heads tripping on Christmas Eve. Computer-generated Ecstasy tablets tumbled across the screen. This was hardly a 'Just Say No' endorsement. The band performed the track live on *Top Of The Pops*, and the nation's televisions took the raves of Ibiza straight into people's homes.

On November 23, 1988, New Order departed from Heathrow Airport for Rio De Janeiro. Always working to keep their live shows exciting and refreshing, they embarked on their first-ever South American tour, all four bandmembers excited to visit a new continent. Michael Shamberg followed them, planning to make a documentary for television, and the party arrived in Rio on November 24, where they held a press conference to introduce themselves to the people. They spent the following two evenings playing at the sixteen-thousand seat Maracanazinho in Brazil. The 27th was a day of rest, then they performed at the Gigantino in Porto Alegre and Ibirapuera in Sao Paolo, where a chaotic rendition of The Velvet Underground's 'Sister Ray' was taped for inclusion on an AIDS relief album, *Like A Girl, I Want You To Keep Coming*. New Order's big finish was to have taken place at a festival marking five years of democracy in Buenos Aires, but a military insurrection made it too dangerous for them to play. The cancellation was especially heartwrenching because it would have featured New Order's largest audience to date: over a hundred thousand souls were expected to attend.

The loss in Buenos Aires was recouped by a triumphant homecoming gig at Manchester's G-Mex Centre. Despite the failure of an Emulator II synthesizer (which meant they'd have to buy a new one soon), New Order thrilled the masses and won the critics with the English début of their new acid-house sound, and Barney, at last, had liberated himself from his overly self-conscious nature. He felt free to dance onstage, while Hooky – whose hair was longer than ever before – waved his bass to and fro, posing, as the message painted on his amplifiers said, like a "guitar Nero". New Order had become entertainers. The public couldn't get enough of them.

With its psychedelic, colourful sleeve, *Technique* proclaimed New Order's love for acid house culture in bold style. It combined all of the genres which had ever influenced them – punk, electronic, hip-hop, acoustic, house – in a comfortable, natural way. And just as the music was fully realised, Barney Sumner sounded in complete control of his voice. He was far removed from the frightened, hesitant singer he'd been in 1980, and his lyrics rivalled Ian Curtis' best for their eloquence and emotional impact. Recently separated from his wife Sue, Barney expressed all his anger, frustration, powerlessness, pride, joy and sadness within his songs. *Technique* stood up under scrutiny and repeated listenings. On all levels, it was the greatest work New Order produced.

'Fine Time' got the party started right off the bat, with sheep baa-ing at different speeds, beats stomping over everything else. 'All The Way' took a step back towards New Order's exclusive brand of guitar-rock, with Barney declaring, "It takes years to find the nerve to be apart from what you've done, to find the truth inside yourself and not depend on anyone." All four bandmembers played as a single entity, moving the song seamlessly from one passage to another.

'Love Less' began with a drumbeat straight out of 'Love Vigilantes', and Barney coughing to clear his throat. Like the sound of him spitting during 'Thieves Like Us', this little detail made 'Love Less' immediate and informal, a conversation from one friend to another. The lyrics were very sad, Barney telling Sue, 'I work hard to give you all the things that you need and almost everything that you see. I spent a lifetime working on you, and

you won't even talk to me.' He sounded on the brink of surrender.

His fighting spirit and New Order's disco sensibilities returned for 'Round & Round', Gillian's keyboards and Hook's bass dancing together. Where he had been tender and begging on 'Love Less', here Barney attacked with spite: 'You can't tell me what's going on and that I am weak while you are strong. What is it you need that makes your heart bleed? Do you really know? 'Cause it doesn't show.' Synthesizers produced an oscillating noise that whirled around and around, hence the title.

'I always know what it takes to make you my lover,' Barney taunted on 'Guilty Partner', and then decided, 'I know that I am okay 'cause you're here with me today' on 'Run.' The singer came across as forthright and honest, not censoring a single thought. He was brave enough to reveal both his sadism and his sympathy. He seemed like a normal, complete human being.

'Mr. Disco' was a fantasy written about a man on vacation in Ibiza who meets the girl of his dreams at an acid house party. He loses track of her, then spends the rest of his life trying to find her again. 'I can't find my peace of mind without you,' Mr. Disco said, tormented. The music was a chipper and bouncy acid house soundtrack which clicked because it was so incompatible with the depressing lyrics. It would have made for a great single, not to mention an incredible video.

'Vanishing Point' and 'Dream Attack' retained the dance music influence, and the verses offered ambiguous visions of agony and ecstasy, but the choruses pulled no punches: 'My life ain't no holiday, I've been through the point of no return. I've seen what a man can do, I've seen all the hate of a woman, too.' Barney's morale plummeted with these lyrics to 'Vanishing Point', the failure of his marriage having wounded him irreparably. But he rose like a phoenix in 'Dream Attack', finding value in his art and himself. 'I can't be owned by no-one, but I want to be with you,' he said. 'I can't be owned by no-one, what am I supposed to do? I can't see the sense in you leaving, all I need is your love to believe in, and for you I will do what I can, but I can't change the way that I am.' The fading melodies radiated strength, not weakness or collapse. He refused to be a victim.

Factory and Qwest took no chances with *Technique*, launching an 'Advertising Technique' campaign of billboards and full-colour ads placed in music and entertainment magazines. They even covered an entire house with promo posters. Doing their part, the bandmembers submitted to media requests for interviews. Nobody involved with this record was willing to let it go unnoticed.

Michael Shamberg completed a video for the track 'Round & Round' on March 3, and the single appeared shortly thereafter in a myriad of remixed forms. Qwest issued seven-inch vinyl and cassette singles featuring 'Round & Round (7" Version)' b/w an edit of the previously unreleased instrumental 'Best And Marsh.' The Qwest 12" single compiled a '12' Version', 'Club Mix', and '12" Remix' of 'Round & Round', plus a longer rendition of 'Best And Marsh'. Factory also released a 12", and made all of the assorted remixes of 'Round & Round' available over two *Round & Remix* CD singles. The first disc had 'Round & Round (7" Version)', 'Round & Round (12" Version)', 'Best And Marsh (7" Version)', and the real jewel, 'Vanishing Point (Instrumental Making Out Mix)', an alternate take of the *Technique* track written for the BBC programme *Making Out*. This would have been the perfect song to end the album; its melodies conveyed emotions even without Barney's touching vocals. The second disc, a tiny CD3, came in a flimsy cardboard package and Warholian sleeve. The 'Club Mix' and '12" Remix' available through Qwest resurfaced here, but the 'Detroit Mix' of 'Round & Round', which recalled '5.8.6.' in execution and arrangement, made this worth purchasing despite the overlapping of material.

By issuing so many versions of the single, New Order reaffirmed its commitment to dance music. DJs could pick a remix that best suited the tastes of an audience, or combine several mixes into a new construction.

New Order also remained enamoured of the stage. The band played the NEC Arena in Birmingham on Easter Sunday, preparing for an extensive North American tour to begin in April. The quartet bought new synthesizers to use on the tour, forcing Stephen, Gillian, and Barney to re-program all of the sound effects they'd created over the years into these new instruments, a long and laborious process which required lots of time. In-between rehearsals, Barney and Johnny Marr practised in the Lake District, writing material for Sell Your Body. The workload must have been a strain on the singer, who was legendary for going about things at a snail's pace. By spreading himself too thinly, Barney was apparently unable to re-program all the sounds in New Order's repertoire into the synths before leaving with the band for America. This limited them to being able only to play tracks they had entered before the deadline: material from *Technique*, their greatest hits, and a few favourite album cuts, like 'Your Silent Face.' New Order's policy of only doing a set number of songs at any performance

to keep concerts from getting monotonous now seemed redundant: lack of preparation forced them to repeat themselves.

The North American tour began in April, with college-radio darlings Throwing Muses opening the shows. At Seattle's Paramount Theater, madness reigned supreme. The opening volley of 'True Faith' and 'Ceremony' was incredible, winding the audience into overdrive. As if the hall's notoriously-domineering security staff wasn't busy enough keeping fans in their seats, Hooky grabbed a would-be stagediver by the face and shoved him back into his chair, shaking his pony-tailed head back and forth as if to say, 'No way, buster!' Smoke and laser beams surrounded New Order from all sides, giving the show a futuristic, acid-house-party ambience. Barney altered a lyric during 'Round & Round' ('What is it you need that makes your pussy bleed?'), and reprimanded the crowd for cheering during the instrumental break at the middle of 'Vanishing Point.' Hooky dragged his index fingers down from his eyes to illustrate the lyric about a weeping demon, and ended the gig alone, sawing a guitar pick into the strings of his bass while twirling dials on his amplifiers, creating a storm of white noise. The band celebrated afterwards by dancing in the Paramount's upstairs dressing room area. The rest of the tour would not go so well.

The second leg of the American tour featured a three-act lineup, as had been used in 1987. New Order joined forces with The Sugarcubes and former Sex Pistol Johnny Rotten's band Public Image Limited, but New Order undeniably sparkled more than their companions. Dubbed 'The Monsters of Alternative Rock' by promoters, the triple-bill hit both coasts (adding rap group De La Soul for a University of San Diego gig) and cut through the heart of America. It concluded at the Meadowlands Arena in New Jersey on July 19, 1989. Entertainment industry gossip claimed New Order earned one and a half million pounds from ticket receipts and merchandise sales – t-shirts, badges, posters, tourbooks, sunglasses – but travelling exhausted the group. Only Peter Hook enjoyed long tours. The other bandmembers, especially Barney Sumner, struggled to feel normal after months away from home, performing in strange cities, surrounded by fans, reporters, and shady characters who attempted to sell them drugs. The group later admitted to drinking as a way of coping, and Barney claimed he took various substances to dispel his confusion and pain.

The group returned to England, where they played the Glastonbury Fair and visited Dry, a new bar Factory opened on Oldham Street in Manchester. Hooky, Gillian, Stephen, and Barney could often be spotted throughout the summer in Dry or the Hacienda, sometimes joined by other famous musicians with whom they were friends. Mancunians embraced New Order and Factory as two of the city's strongest allies. Whereas Manchester had once been in decline, investments in these hometown businesses such as Dry evinced a regional pride, and lent the area an image as an internationally-fashionable and exciting place to be. New Order became local heroes.

New versions of the *Technique* song 'Run' appeared on a limited-edition 12" single released through Factory during the first week of September. Producer Scott Litt created 'Run 2' and 'Run 2 (Extended Mix)' out of the album track, and also worked on the B-sides, 'MTO' and 'MTO (Minus Mix)'. Only twenty thousand copies of the disc were printed, most of which disappeared from record stores instantly. The video for 'Run 2', using footage taken during the tour, was directed by Robert Frank, best known for making The Rolling Stones movie 'Cocksucker Blues'. Qwest never released the single or video in America, much to fans' dismay.

A New Order 'Substance' videocassette did come out in most countries two weeks later. It collected 'Confusion', the unedited cut of 'The Perfect Kiss', 'Shellshock' (a patchwork of outtakes from the 'Perfect Kiss' video shoot, plus Stephen Morris' home movies), 'Bizarre Love Triangle', 'True Faith', 'Touched By the Hand of God', and 'Blue Monday 1988', all linked together by animated sequences choreographed to the tune of 'The Happy One'. This was a great collection, remarkable not only for its content but for the assembly of great directors who'd worked on the videos. Had it included the short for the original 'Blue Monday', as well as 'Fine Time', 'Round & Round' and 'Run 2', 'Substance' would have been faultless, but as a document of New Order's best clips made prior to *Technique*, it was invaluable.

Peter Hook, Barney Sumner, Gillian Gilbert and Stephen Morris all worked on solo projects in the fall of 1989. Michael Shamberg flew to England to work with Steve and Gillian on the theme song for *America's Most Wanted*, the Fox network's TV show profiling fugitive criminals. Shamberg produced the opening montage (it recalled the video for 'Bizarre Love Triangle'), which the New Order duo scored with a tense synthesizer instrumental. The sound and images aptly conveyed fear and danger, well suited to the content of the show.

New Order ┼ Joy Division

Now calling themselves Electronic, Barney Sumner and Johnny Marr reunited in Manchester to write more songs together. They told record cover designer Mark Farrow that they were in the market for collaborators, and Farrow told his clients The Pet Shop Boys about the cattle call. The Pet Shop Boys, singer Neil Tennant and keyboardist Chris Lowe, contacted Electronic, and all four of them met in a recording studio to listen to an instrumental track Sumner and Marr had written. Everyone agreed Tennant and Sumner ought to sing on the track as a duet, so they laid down the vocals on a tune they would eventually call 'Getting Away With It'.

Former ABC drummer and current member of The The (with Johnny Marr) David Palmer played drums on the track, and The Art of Noise's Anne Dudley created a string arrangement. When completed, 'Getting Away With It' emerged as stunning pop music; the all-star lineup of members of New Order, The Smiths, The Pet Shop Boys, ABC and The Art of Noise invited cries of 'Supergroup!', but this was no lazy troupe of wealthy musicians churning out ill-conceived songs during a holiday. 'Getting Away With It' began softly, guitars, keyboards, voices and classical instruments slowly

Electronic: Barney and Johnny Marr.

woven together. When the chorus came along, the listener was already hypnotised, and the duet between Barney and Neil Tennant embedded itself into every mind that heard it: "Whatever I do, it's clear to see that I love you more than you love me." Eventually, everything faded away but Anne Dudley's strings, which tied a neat little bow around 'Getting Away With It', making it mandatory for holiday wish lists. A second Electronic/Pet Shop Boys collaboration, 'Patience Of A Saint', would not match the magnificence of 'Getting Away With It', but for one brief moment, the musicians created a masterpiece to match anything written during the decade. 'Getting Away With It' was the last great pop song of the Eighties.

Barney Sumner, Johnny Marr, Neil Tennant and Chris Lowe went to dinner at the end of the recording sessions, and they invited Gillian Gilbert, Stephen Morris, and Rob Gretton to dine with them. They chose to eat at a restaurant which, unknown to them, had a dress code, and the *maître'd* stopped them at the door, telling them that they weren't wearing the right clothing. Tennant said, "Drop him," i.e. let him know we are celebrities. Gretton thought he meant "Bribe him", and Sumner thought he meant "Punch him", and a riot nearly erupted in the lobby. Finally, a customer told the *maître'd* to relax his standards and seven of the most important people in the British music industry sat down for a meal.

Peter Hook kept busy as well, producing (and partying with) The Stone Roses, and recording a self-titled EP with his group Revenge. Factory released a 12" and a CD by the band in the winter. The 12" began with '7 Reasons', a bouncy track which could have fitted comfortably on *Brotherhood*. Hook's voice had improved immensely since he sang lead on 'Dreams Never End', and as a lyricist, he vacillated between articulate sensitivity – "It's good to be young and gifted again, to see if it all happens twice" – to contrived, goofy nastiness – "I'm gonna get it and crush it through your head 'till all the pain's gone and you are dead." Another line – "Who wants to be adored?" – seemed like a response to The Stone Roses track 'I Wanna Be Adored'. Hook's lyrics drew from a very specific number of topics for inspiration, often focusing on God, religion, love, lust, childhood, the Sun, Heaven and Hell. He expressed his thoughts in impressionistic sketches, not telling a story so much as creating scenes and moods, much like Barney had done in his formative years as a singer.

Revenge's music strived at various times for power or gentleness, mixing heavy metal and disco more aggressively than New Order (Revenge's next-of-kin would more likely have been *Turbo*-era Judas Priest). The band's first attempts at a grand statement, 'Jesus... I Love You' and its dub mix, 'I Love You Too', were obviously modelled on one of Hook's favourite New Order tracks, 'The Perfect Kiss'. Unfortunately, Revenge lost control of the song; the trio filled it with every manner of effect and interlude to the detriment of its cohesiveness.

'Jesus... I Love You (7" Edit)' on the *Revenge* CD offered the true form of the song. Stripped of rambling instrumental sections, this short version concentrated its power and exploded like a firecracker. Hook's excitement about being in Revenge, as he expressed in '7 Reasons', now seemed justified. That song, plus the unedited 'Jesus... I Love You', also appeared on the CD, as well as an exclusive instrumental track, 'Bleachboy'.

The EP's sleeve began a group tradition of using sexy female models on record covers. These 'Revenge Girls' were inspired by *Skin Two*'s in-house models, the 'Avenger Girls'. Hook loved the look of fetishwear – often insisting, perhaps too innocently, that he did not practise sadomasochism – and he hired *Skin Two* photographer Trevor Watson to take the cover photo of a playfully dishevelled woman caressing leather car seats. Sadly, not many people got beyond looking at the sleeve to explore the music within, and some who heard Revenge could not accept the notion that hard rock and dance music weren't mutually exclusive. The *Revenge* EP sat in record stores, unappreciated by many except the Peter Hook fans who tracked it down.

'Getting Away With It' by Electronic became the New Order solo project to win most people's hearts and attentions. Offered in an assortment of remixes, the song bounded up the charts and earned considerable airplay in England and America. The liquor glass on the cover reflected Electronic's clean, rich, luxurious sound, far removed from Revenge's techno growl. The instrumental B-side, 'Lucky Bag', recalled *Technique*-era New Order, especially 'Vanishing Point'. Qwest conveniently released all of the available mixes on a CD single in early 1990.

The video for 'Getting Away With It' broke Barney's long-held taboo against lip-synching. The plotless, lifeless film of Marr, Tennant and Sumner pretending to play and sing certainly did not match New Order's imaginative clips, making it hard to understand why Barney would compromise his principles for such a mediocre production. For him to lower his standards so early in Electronic's career did not bode well for the band's future.

1989 had been a good year for New Order. Despite the quartet's disgust with touring, they'd released their greatest LP to date and had been rewarded by critics and fans. *Technique* earned Factory Records a lot of money (some of which probably helped pay for the Dry bar), as did the album *Bummed* by Happy Mondays. For the first time ever, a Factory band rivalled New Order and Joy Division in popularity. The Mondays' cheery, E-powered dance music took England by storm in 1989, and their single 'Wrote For Luck' emerged as the foremost anthem of acid house culture. 'Wrote For Luck' and *Bummed* were both produced by former Factory director Martin Hannett. Tony Wilson considered the LP Hannett's best work since *Closer.* "(Hannett) became a very ill man," Wilson said of the producer's years away from Factory. "He became a real down and out, and just surfaced with a brilliant album (*Bummed*). We're friends again." Hannett had returned while New Order had splintered into three component parts, but the band would not be apart for long.

Revenge played its début gig at the Hacienda Temperance Club in Paris on July 25, 1990. Hook, Hicks and C.J. were joined onstage by a second bassist named David Potts and a drummer known only as Ash. Their set included material from the band's forthcoming LP, which was recorded at Suite 16 and scheduled for release in late March, later pushed back to June. This delay may have been caused by Peter Hook's reunion with Stephen Morris, Gillian Gilbert, and Bernard Sumner to record 'World In Motion', the official World Cup theme song for the English football team. New Order first tried recording it with producer and The The collaborator Roli Mosiman at Real World studios, but weren't satisfied with the results. They brought in Stephen Hague for another session, this one more to their liking.

Traditionally, a World Cup team would always sing on the recording of its theme song, and 'World In Motion' was no exception. Footballers Peter Beardsley, Paul 'Gazza' Gascoigne, Steve McMahon, Chris Waddle, Des Walker and John Barnes all sang the chorus – "We're singing for England: En-ger-land!" – and Barnes performed a solo rap written by comedian Keith Allen, a rap which denounced hooliganism and likened the acid house virtues of peace and love to soccer: "Express yourself, it's one on one." New Order admired the team's ability to consume alcohol during the session, and were very happy with the way the re-recorded 'World In Motion' turned out.

Revenge embarked on a tour in mid-April, starting at an S & M party organised by *Skin Two* stylist Francisca Malan. The band hit a number of small clubs in Scotland and England, including King Tut's Wah-Wah Hut in

Below: Peter Hook on stage with Revenge.

Glasgow, and the Leadmill in Sheffield, where a pre-gig interview with *Melody Maker*'s Jon Wilde overran with Hooky's favourite sayings, "Fuck off" and "You cunt". The press had branded Hook a "rock and roll Viking" because of his long hair, scruffy beard, leather trousers and Harley Davidson t-shirts, and just as Joy Division once taunted critics by playing up to Nazi rumours, Hook was glad to fulfil the media's misconception of him. The doting father of two (Iris had recently given birth to a son, Jack) named *Spartacus* and *The Vikings* as two of his favourite films, and shouted at ticketholders who asked for autographs or information about the future of New Order. Shortly after the *Melody Maker* piece appeared on news stands, the magazine ran a transcript of an imaginary phoneline, "It's Your Line To Peter Hook". The hilarious, fictitious conversations between Hook ("Fuck off, you cunt!") and a succession of terrified fans illustrated the bassist's wildman persona, and Hooky liked it so much that he cut it out and taped it on the wall at Suite 16. However, his play acting did not sit well with every fan of New Order and Revenge. Hooky seemed to forget his comments could be taken seriously and might hurt people's feelings. Revenge no doubt lost some listeners because of Hook's namecalling.

He didn't spare bandmates Dave Hicks and C.J. either, often taunting them in public. During one concert, Hook shoved his hand down the back of Hicks' trousers to embarrass him onstage, and during an interview, urinated into a beermug and tried to force him to drink his pee. Yet he always made a point of giving Hicks and Jones equal opportunity to speak to the media. Hook knew that most journalists only cared to hear his opinions, and he would sometimes only talk once his bandmates had their say. If Hook had spoken first, reporters might have hung up the phone without bothering with the other members of Revenge. Hook maintained that the trio was a democracy, all three members equally important. The contradictions of Revenge – a hard rock band which played synthesizers, led by a thoughtful and intelligent bassist who enjoyed his tough-guy image – were the band's unique features and the biggest hindrances preventing them from attracting a massive audience.

Below: With actor/
comedian Keith Allen and
footballer John Barnes.

The second Revenge release, 'Pineapple Face', came out through Factory on April 30. Despite the title, this throbbing, bass heavy tale of erotic yearning had nothing to do with deposed Panamanian dictator Manuel Noriega. The suite-like track burst at the seams with melodies, hooklines and musical passages, including the chorus of Abba's 'S.O.S.', which may or may not have been used consciously. The 12" coupled two remixes, 'Pineapple Face's Big Day' and 'Pineapple Face's Revenge' with the quiet, reflective '14K', centred around Hicks' guitar and Hook's breathy vocals. The lyrics continued in Revenge's style of sin and redemption.

Capitol released a cassette, 12", and CD single of 'Pineapple Face' on May 16. The tape offered 'Pineapple Face's Edit' (a short version of the song), '14K' and 'Pineapple Face's Big Day', while the 12" added 'Pineapple Face (LP Version)' and 'Pineapple Face Calls It A Day'. The CD included all of the above, and added 'Bleachboy'. The 'Edit' and 'LP Version' proved 'Pineapple Face' to be much heavier than the original Factory single suggested, and CD sound revealed previously inaudible melodies and rhythm tracks. At over half an hour in length, the bargain-priced EP truly was a bargain.

Hook's status as a member of New Order was a very valuable tool in marketing Revenge to the media and the listening public, and Capitol didn't hesitate to promote the band as "Revenge featuring Peter Hook". The company even sent a four-track promo CD to radio stations labelled as such. The CD offered 'Pineapple Face's Edit', 'Pineapple Face's Big Day', 'Pineapple Face Calls It a Day', and the rare 'Pineapple Face's Big Day (Edit)'. In trying to make 'Pineapple Face's Big Day' short enough to get radio airplay, editor Carl Segal removed entire sections of the song. The final product hardly represented the original.

Peter Hook starred in the video for 'Pineapple Face', but "equally important" band members Dave Hooks and Chris Jones didn't even appear in cameo roles. The clip, filmed in L.A. at considerable expense, began with Hook repairing his motorcycle and donning a necklace bearing the key to his chastity belt. Two Revenge Girls, a blonde dominatrix and a submissive brunette, united in an empty factory for a secret tryst, which was interrupted by a third woman wielding a small propane torch (a parody of Sigourney Weaver brandishing a flame-thrower in *Aliens*). She disappeared into a fog as strangely as she arrived, then Hook appeared, the final member of this bizarre love triangle. In a brilliant scene which shattered the macho stereotypes so prevalent in music videos, both girls caressed Hook's chest, then ripped the necklace from his neck, letting it – and the key to the chastity belt – slip through a grating on the floor. The film closed with Hook on his knees, clawing the ground in frustration.

The sexually-charged imagery of 'Pineapple Face' was too hot for MTV. Although some regional programmes broadcast this "R-Rated" version, a "PG-13" version also failed to garner much national airplay, which was just as well: by rearranging scenes into a dreamlike hodgepodge, the censored 'Pineapple Face' not only lost its raunchiness, it also lost its power and its message. The single didn't get the airplay it deserved, either, but 'Pineapple Face' did find an audience in dance clubs.

Peter Saville's sleeve for 'Pineapple Face' used a close-up photo of a Revenge Girl wearing a metallic bikini apparently purchased straight out of a *Skin Two* mail order catalogue. It was taken by *Playboy* photographer (and former centrefold) Suze Randall. Saville printed the titles in a very ritzy typeface often used on the cover of *Vogue* magazine. The high-fashion look of Revenge covers set the band apart from Joy Division and New Order's stark, classical designs, just as the music of Revenge possessed an identity all its own. The press, however, branded Revenge a pale imitation of New Order because both groups featured Hook's distinctive style of playing bass. And despite Hook's insistence that Hicks and Jones were his equals, the duo were rarely given as much coverage in articles, and their faces were often cropped from photographs. Fourteen years in the public eye had toughened Hook to criticism, but his bandmates were devastated when people slammed Revenge. Hook's optimism and love for the group may have been the only thing to keep Revenge together after the first, punishing volleys from the press.

New Order and the English World Cup team met during the first days of May to film a video for 'World In Motion', and Barney Sumner startled everyone by arriving on the set in an Elvis-style karate suit, both a joke and an admission that New Order had become pop stars. The band and athletes, functioning under the name EnglandNewOrder, linked arms for the finale, singing the chorus like a bunch of giddy old men in a tavern. The following week, the single itself shot to the top of the charts with no resistance. The irony that a lightweight football anthem would go to number one where 'Love Will Tear Us Apart', 'The Perfect Kiss', 'Temptation', and 'Atmosphere' had not wasn't lost on the band. As they admitted, 'World In Motion' would probably scare off the last Joy Division fans because it was so upbeat and happy. Even Peter Saville got into the mood of the record by designing a sleeve depicting the Earth as a giant

Peter Hook with Revenge.

soccer ball. The populist 'World In Motion' earned New Order an audience of non-standard music listeners, especially sports enthusiasts. Peter Hook's mother went on record as saying she was more proud of her son doing the football song than of any of his other accomplishments.

Almost as if to temper the band's happiness, the BBC complained that 'World In Motion' resembled the theme song New Order had composed for the TV show *Reportage*. "I'd like it to be recognised that the 'Reportage' theme was written by New Order and not by the BBC producers," Stephen Morris said in a press release. The BBC retreated from the issue.

The Hacienda became accepted as the heart of acid house culture in the spring and summer of 1990. News crews arrived from around the world to "Madchester," interviewing Tony Wilson and filming dancers who wore oversized smiley-face t-shirts and bell-bottomed trousers. Like the Electric Circus before it, the Hacienda also came to the attention of local authorities. The Greater Manchester Police threatened to shut down the club because of drug use on Hacienda premises, and the club issued a statement, saying, "We believe that we have done everything within our power to remove drug use from our club. Over the past year, we have co-operated fully with the Greater Manchester Police, attending and instigating meetings and implementing all police suggestions. People have been ejected from the club, and the GMP have been able to make several related arrests and subsequent convictions.

"Over the coming weeks, we will continue to extend our offer of full co-operation to the GM in our joint efforts to combat the problem.

"In the light of what we believe have been major successes in this campaign, we are now redoubling our efforts to remove all traces of soft drug use in order to secure the future of the most vital music venue in Europe." The no-drugs door policy established by the Hacienda led to clientèle being refused entry at the door or being escorted outside by bouncers, and sometimes, so many people were denied access to the club that it was half-full on traditionally busy nights. The GMP continued its opposition to the Hacienda, going so far as to combat the renewal of the club's business licence. Lawyer George Carmen was hired to represent the nightclub in court.

The Hacienda celebrated its eighth birthday on May 21, and all four members of New Order, plus Johnny Marr, Dave Hicks, Chris Jones, A Certain Ratio and Happy Mondays attended the party. Searchlights beamed into the night sky, and drugs were noticeably absent, for fear of a police crackdown. Unfortunately, contraband still leaked into the club, violent gangs fought to control the drug market, and before summer ended, the Hacienda would suffer its first death: sixteen-year-old Claire Leighton died of apparent heat exhaustion from dancing and taking Ecstasy. She over-exerted herself, her body temperature soared, and she literally boiled. This cast a pall over the ravers who had trumpeted Ecstasy as a non-dangerous drug.

Four remixes of 'World In Motion' appeared in mid-June, 'The Subbuteo Mix', 'The Subbuteo Dub', 'The Call the Carabinieri Mix' and 'The No Alla Violenza Mix'. All of these, plus both sides of the original Factory 12", were released in America spread over a CD single and cassette maxi-single.

Factory channelled its profits from 'World In Motion' into a new corporate headquarters which it had purchased the year before for £100,000. The company then invested over £500,000 to refurbish the interior, a stylish piece of work designed by Ben Kelly including television monitors playing MTV every hour of the day (much to Barney's disgust) and a boardroom table suspended from the ceiling by wires. Money flowed quickly for a time, but considering the GMP's threats against Factory's cash

cow the Hacienda, this investment probably should have waited until everything was smoothed out in court. The Factory directors should also have considered the re-sale value of their new HQ; the remodelling suited their own aesthetic needs, but most other companies would have found these offices unusable. Factory might have difficulty selling the building if it ever needed money at short notice.

The Revenge début album came out on Capitol on June 12, 1990, and on Factory six days later. Entitled *One True Passion*, it featured the requisite bevy of Revenge Girls in the CD booklet, as well as a photo of the band itself: the first occurrence of a group portrait of New Order or one of its splinter factions ever appearing on an internationally-available release.

One True Passion opened with 'Pineapple Face', Hook singing, "I'm trying an icy form of love" while machines chattered around him. These blips and whistles would swarm throughout *One True Passion*, but where Revenge once wrote 'Jesus... I Love You' around such effects, here they used them to accentuate moods and lyrics. For example, the Morse-code beeping at the start of 'Big Bang' intensified the intro's loneliness. The words enigmatically connected this track to an older one, Hook saying, "Now I know that if I try, there's seven reasons." But the most stirring verse said, "This time I'll try the shining path of sin". Hook could turn quite a phrase.

"Thought of you as my mirror to show me the state of myself," he said in 'Kiss The Chrome', which allegedly was about running over people with cars. The lyrics and music told a different story; one of emotional dependence. 'Slave' didn't live up to the S&M connotations of its title, either. Spectral voices faded in and out while the music pounded and roared. "Nothing ever lasts forever," Hook said, "and it's the same for you, I'm sure." After an excerpt of a telephone call, 'Bleachboy' appeared with lyrics added as 'Bleachman', Hook bragging, "I killed a man with a knife, kept it pure and simple for his kids and his wife." Then he admitted, "I'm a liar." This condensed Hook's Viking image perfectly; it was all a show, all put-on. The sounds C.J. crammed into 'Bleachman' demanded headphones, because there were far too many piled one over the other to be heard under normal listening conditions. They made the song epic.

'Surf Nazi' was named after the B-movie 'Surf Nazis Must Die'. It offered a Hicks and Hook duet, as well as snippets of in-the studio dialogue. '7 Reasons' appeared in remixed form on CD copies of *One True Passion*, followed by 'Fag Hag', a derogatory term for heterosexual women who would rather have gay men as friends rather than straights. Maybe playing off the idea of the Sea Hag in Popeye cartoons, Hooky sang a sea shanty in a gruff baritone: "Oh, we don't know where we're going and we don't know where we've been, we are bonny, lovely sailors and we're headed off to sea." The thunderous drums were similar to the ones used in 'Slave', and as a joke, Hook played the bassline of 'Murder'. Thanks to such funny touches, and an unforgettable chorus, 'Fag Hag' may have been the most rewarding song on the LP. Revenge ended the song cycle with the beautiful 'It's Quiet'. Hook's 'echoey' vocals, Hick's acoustic guitar, and Jones' simple keyboard melodies acted as a delicate counterpoint to the powerful anthems which preceded this song, and the final lyric exposed the source of Hook's inner strength: "What they do where I come from is laugh at life, admit you're wrong." Having travelled the globe in search of unknown pleasures, the narrator returned home bruised, humbled, happy and wise. And Peter Hook emerged from behind his bass and his image as an articulate poet.

One True Passion was an extraordinary début, and Revenge toured to promote the album. They began in England in late June, hitting Windsor and London, then Edinburgh, Aberdeen and Greenock in Scotland before embarking on a European tour. When this ended, Hook, Tony Wilson, and 'World In Motion' co-writer Keith Allen flew to the New Music Seminar in Manhattan during the first week of July. Wilson and Allen – who posed as a drug-pushing psychologist – spoke at 'Wake Up, America, You're Dead', a discussion about the future of dance music, and the two men initiated a shouting match between pro-American and pro-English conventioneers. Hook spoke on the artists' panel (and had his picture taken with the Partridge Family's David Cassidy and soul singer Barry White), which itself fell apart as East- and West-Coast rappers attacked each other.

Hook returned to England and Revenge, performing several dates until the tour's conclusion at the International 1 in Manchester. Then he and the band travelled America in an extremely low-key manner during August.

Barney Sumner kept busy as well. He mixed two 'Rockin' Over Manchester Hacienda' versions of 'Rockin' Over the Beat' by Technotronic, as well as 'Can't Stop Loving You' by A Certain Ratio. He also stood by Electronic, continuing to write songs with Johnny Marr. They surprised everyone by accepting Depeche Mode's invitation to open two gigs at Dodgers' Stadium in Los Angeles. Few other bands would have chosen to play for the first time before audiences of sixty thousand people, but Electronic hoped to make every show an event.

The concerts took place on the first weekend of August. Marr and Sumner were joined by The Pet Shop Boys and backup musicians Kesta Martinez, Andrew Robinson, A Certain Ratio's Donald Johnson, and according to some reports, David Palmer. Barney suffered from pre-gig jitters which left him ill, and he couldn't remember all of the lyrics to the songs (in part because he was writing some up until showtime), but despite these troubles, Electronic gave an energetic performance, highlighted by 'Patience Of A Saint', 'Getting Away With It', and the new 'Get The Message'. The audience had only ever heard 'Getting Away With It', and only Barney was unrestrained by instruments (or attitude) to dance on stage, but the crowd, which included fans of New Order, The Smiths, and The Pet Shop Boys, were appreciative. Without an Ian Curtis or Peter Hook by his side, Barney found himself the centre of attention. He wasn't comfortable being so much in the limelight, yet the results were satisfying. Electronic considered releasing a live LP of the gig in favour of the studio album they'd struggled so long to complete, but scrapped the idea. After two shows before probably more people than Joy Division had ever played to during their entire career, Electronic went back to Manchester where they recorded in hermit-like seclusion.

The second and final single off *One True Passion* came in late summer. For Revenge, it had been a choice between 'Kiss The Chrome' and 'Slave'. They chose 'Slave', issuing a dozen different remixes, and three B-sides ('Jesus... I Love You (7" Edit)', the nicely made 'Kiss the Chrome (7" Edit)', and a dull cover of John Cale's 'Amsterdam') over three different 12" singles, a CD single, and a cassette. Several of the 'Slave' remixes added raps by producer Daddy-O, and the result was laughable. The original version remained the best, and the general public ignored the singles, maybe with justifiable cause.

New Order were scheduled to regroup in November to work on an LP, but Barney's side projects distracted him. He wrote music to be played at London's Decorative Arts Group in London during an exhibition by Central Station Design, the creators of sleeves for Happy Mondays. He also sang 'Spanish Heart' with the dance group 808 State, and recorded 'Good Together' with A Certain Ratio and Happy Mondays vocalist Shaun Ryder at Johnny Marr's home studio in Manchester. Sumner and Marr also joined The Banderas, a Scottish/English duo, for 'This Is Your Life', produced by Stephen Hague. Electronic continued to work on their now legendary LP, although many doubted it would ever be released. New Order remained on ice, but at the time, there was no reason to think it would be long before they resurfaced. The wait turned out to be far longer than even the band had expected.

In early January, 1991, the Hacienda's court case was settled, with the club being granted a six-month reprieve in which to prevent drugs from entering the premises. Electronic celebrated the announcement with a secret gig there, which was attended by a number of Factory luminaries, including Peter Hook, Stephen Morris and Gillian Gilbert. Neil Tennant MC'd the show, introducing Barney Sumner, Johnny Marr, Donald Johnson, Andy Robinson, and Kesta Martinez to an excited crowd. A brief, buoyant set by Electronic restored everyone's faith in the future of the nightspot, but unfortunately, that faith was misplaced.

On January 26, 1991, just as on every night for the past couple of months, the Hacienda's bouncers went about their routine of ejecting anyone who was using drugs or causing a disturbance within the club. They approached one troublesome patron, and the man reacted by pulling out a machine-gun. New Order and Tony Wilson decided that such a blatant show of force was an omen of worse things to come, and on January 31, they held a press conference to announce that the Hacienda was closing down.

Peter Hook, Stephen Morris, Bernard Sumner and Gillian Gilbert looked on as Wilson said, "The Hacienda is closing its doors as of today. It is with the greatest reluctance that for the moment, we are turning the lights out on what is, for us, a most important place. We are forced into taking this drastic action in order to protect our employees, our members and all our clients. We are quite simply sick and tired of dealing with instances of personal violence.

"We hope, and we must believe, that we can re-open the Hacienda in a better climate. But until we are able to run the club in a safe manner and in a way that the owners believe will guarantee the role of the Hacienda at the heart of the city's youth community, it is with great sadness that we will be shutting down our club."

New Order issued a "no comment", preferring to stand by Wilson's statement. Several Hacienda employees were laid off, the manager met with city officials to plan a course of action, and engineers installed metal detectors for when the club re-opened. The closure cost Factory £200,000.

The Banderas' 'This Is Your Life' and ACR's *4 For the Floor* EP featuring 'Good Together' came out in early February, and 808 State's *Ex.El* with 'Spanish Heart' was issued on March 4. Factory scheduled a March 25 release of a new single by Electronic, but the date was pushed back to April. No new songs by Electronic had been released in over a year. Considering the impression they had made with 'Getting Away With It', and the time they were spending to record a follow-up, the duo were under keen pressure to release a masterpiece.

Select magazine issued *The Factory Tape*, a sampler featuring Electronic's 'Lucky Bag (Miami Edit)', a new Stephen Hague remix of New Order's 'Bizarre Love Triangle', and a David Bianco remix of Revenge's 'Big Bang', with female vocals added. The band must not have liked this cut, because they re-named it 'The Trouble With Girls'. *Heaven And Hell Volume 2*, an album of Velvet Underground cover versions, also included a Revenge song; their take of 'White Light, White Heat'. These would be the last recordings to use the original Hook/Hicks/Jones lineup. Dave Hicks left in March citing "personal and artistic differences" with his bandmates, and formed a new group with the former manager of The Cult. It was hard not to wonder if Peter Hook's teasing and antics had been the motivation for Hicks' departure.

Perhaps to mark the change in Revenge, perhaps simply because he had gotten sick of looking like Erik the Red, Peter Hook shaved off his beard and got a crewcut similar to the one he'd had as a member of Joy Division. Hook sported this new hairdo at Revenge's latest concerts, starting with a gig in Wolverhampton which was sponsored by *Skin Two* magazine and stipulated, "a strict dress code of rubber, leather, fetish glamour or full evening dress". The band added 'Dreams Never End' and The Velvet Underground's sadomasochistic 'Venus In Furs' to their live set, and the press began to support the new Revenge. This was ironic, considering that bad reviews had damaged Hicks' confidence in the first place. The band played throughout England, premièring songs like 'Deadbeat', which revealed an even fiercer sound than ever before. Peter Hook didn't care if anyone liked his band, he just wanted to rock and roll.

New Order, Happy Mondays, and especially Tony Wilson were devastated in April by the news that Martin Hannett had died. The forty-two year old producer had been going to a doctor for some time because of health problems, and on April 17 he died in his sleep of a heart attack. He was survived by a wife and two children.

The death of the man who had, despite years of arguing, helped Factory become a success did not pass unnoticed. The label itself began organising tributes to him, and fans felt the loss of yet another person involved with Joy Division's unique magic. This knowledge tainted their glee at the release of Electronic's 'Get The Message' b/w the instrumental 'Free Will', which had come out just two days before Hannett passed away. Vocalist Denise Johnson provided stunning backup vocals to the A-side, which shone but did not match the brilliance of 'Getting Away With It', and Andrew Robinson programmed computers for the electro wind-up on the flip (Johnson and Robinson were reunited soon afterwards on A Certain Ratio's 'Loosen Up Your Mind', released through Rob Gretton's new personal label, Rob's Records).

The lyrics to 'Get The Message' would have fitted easily on *Technique*, directed as they were to an alienated lover, perhaps Barney's wife, Sue: "When you go away I start to weep, you're too expensive, girl, to keep." The video, however, took a different tack, showing Electronic and hordes of children in the poverty-stricken Philippines to express "living in sin". The opening shot of the band at the mouth of a volcano almost cost Johnny Marr his life; Barney saved him from nearly falling in after a helicopter blinded them both by kicking up volcanic ash. Two remixes of "Get The Message" came out in the first days of May, the 'Groove Mix' and 'Sin Mix' by producers DNA pumping up the rhythm tracks but stripping away Marr's guitar bite. This trade-off for the sake of the dance floor worked commercially if not artistically, as 'Get The Message' became a top club hit.

Whereas Revenge were committed to playing rock with a disco influence, Electronic used the opposite formula: dance music with guitars in a supporting role. Whether or not New Order fans liked either solo act depended on what it was they had liked about the original band. Hooky's bass lines had been as much of a New Order trademark as Barney's vocals. Gillian's idiosyncratic melding of classical and pop music sensibilities and Stephen's live drums were qualities that neither spinoff could declare as their own. Electronic and Revenge were strong, enjoyable entities, and Steve and Gillian's TV scores always delighted, but the New Order sound remained an elusive product of all four musicians working together.

The Hacienda reopened on May 10. Steve and Gillian mingled with Happy Mondays, A Certain Ratio, and 808 State, as well as hundreds of club members glad to return to Manchester's most famous nightspot. Months of closure and remodelling had cost the company both in resources and popularity. The re-opening drew a full house, but some customers were

apparently disappointed with the new-look Hacienda, defecting to other clubs or leaving the scene entirely. Little over a month into its new life, six Hacienda doormen wearing bulletproof vests were stabbed in the legs during an argument with ruffians outside the club. A Happy Mondays gig in Paris was cancelled for fear of violence, and several outdoor raves were called off due to poor ticket sales. Acid house culture and its sense of community had been destroyed by drug wars. Wisely, Electronic went around reminding journalists to pronounce the band's name as El-ectronic, not E-lectronic, lest the drug connotations give people the wrong impression.

Electronic's self-titled début album came out in June, and it immediately soared into the Top Ten. The cover art by Johnson Panas depicted Sumner and Marr on a futuristic TV screen, with the credits printed in a computerised typeface. It was a bald, unimaginative look, hardly as involving as New Order or Joy Division's minimalist sleeves, or even as fitting and distinct as Revenge's hedonistic portraits. *Electronic* blurred into every other pop record on the shelves that summer. Only the music therein would distinguish it – most of the time – from others.

'Idiot Country' protested at police raids on acid house parties, predicting to the youth of England that, "If we got our hands on this nation, we could do what we wanted to do." Electronic got funky on 'Reality', Barney telling a lady, "I don't need you any more, I'm not the man you're looking for." He seemed as obsessive about love as he had been on *Technique*, but the music here didn't do justice to his statements. 'Tighten Up' sounded like an outtake from the Propaganda album *A Secret Wish* until Johnny Marr's guitar kicked in, when it took a turn for the better. "I used to run away but I can't no more," went the chorus, as Barney confronted his enemies. "I'm never gonna do what you want me to." He obviously had not lost his spunk.

Chris Lowe and Neil Tennant appeared on 'The Patience Of A Saint', a midnight drive along fields inhabited by nocturnal insects (the sound of chirping crickets was audible at various times in the song). Barney linked this track to 'World In Motion' through the phrase "talking one on one", and asked of his problems, "Why should I care? I'd rather watch drying paint. And I would try the patience of a saint." The song was so laid back it nearly fell over. Electronic could switch gears, going from high energy to delicious, slothlike laziness, but they had to exercise this talent with care. By not pacing themselves well, the album's momentum would peter out prematurely.

Although Factory skipped over 'Getting Away With It' for the British pressing of *Electronic*, Warner Brothers included it as track five of the American release. Placing both of The Pet Shop Boys songs side by side was a great touch; 'Getting Away With It' deserved to be heard again, and it kept Neil Tennant's sudden appearance on 'Patience Of A Saint' from sounding out of place. 'Gangster' bore the massive keyboard sound of New Order singles like 'Shellshock' and 'Touched By the Hand Of God', and it also presented one of Barney's best character studies to date. The song he had been working on since 1986, 'Gangster' was the imaginary monologue of a young convict, locked in jail before receiving an education or a decent job. "So don't you ever say that we're the same," the hoodlum growled, old and jaded at an early age.

The instrumental 'Soviet' began side two, summoning mental images of hard Russian living and the Cold War. Then 'Get The Message' followed, jingling guitars and thumping rhythms contrasting wonderfully with 'Soviet"s solemn, repressed keyboards. 'Try All You Want' had the kind of melody and lyric one would imagine Sumner could do while clipping his toenails. The midsection was stuffed with improvised effects, many of which were interesting, but none of which belonged. In essence, this was

Electronic's 'Jesus... I Love You'; an overindulgent exercise which severely needed trimming.

Oboist Helen Powell's work on 'Some Distant Memory' elevated what may have otherwise been a charmless dance track. The spiralling, psychedelic music was punctuated by laughter, showing that the band were having quite a time in the studio. For 'Feel Every Beat', the last track on *Electronic*, Barney sniffed to catch his breath, then lit into his first rap song! As if to explain himself, he sang, "If all this seems to be eccentric, be aware, be sure I meant it." The many keyboard and guitar tracks disappeared from the backbeat, which itself was chopped off in a flash and gone. The ending was abrupt and unsatisfying. Something seemed to be missing.

The biggest failure of *Electronic* was one of pacing. Side A should have been side B, and vice versa. That way, 'Soviet' would clear the listener's head in anticipation of the music to follow, and 'Gangster', which must have been important to Sumner for him to have laboured on it for so long, would've left people thinking about the lyrics. 'Feel Every Beat' was a fine song, but it was too lightweight to leave much of an impression. *Electronic* didn't offer a sense of growth and newfound wisdom the way *Closer*, *Technique*, and *One True Passion* had. It simply ended. With 'Gangster' coming last, that problem could have been rectified. After arriving on the scene with such promise, Electronic seemed as mortal and fallible as any band.

Barney Sumner and Johnny Marr attended a Pet Shop Boys gig in Blackpool a few days after the LP's release, but did not appear onstage with them. Electronic did, however, sign aboard for *Cities In The Park*, two nights of concerts organised by Factory, "In Memoriam Martin Hannett". A share of the proceeds were to benefit African Famine Relief and the Kurdish Trust Fund. The first night, Saturday, August 3, l99l, included a number of pop bands, some of whom backed out for reasons known only to themselves. The second night, Sunday, August 4, featured nothing but Factory acts and their associates, including Electronic, Revenge, De La Soul, A Certain Ratio, 808 State, and headliners Happy Mondays. The presence of Electronic and Revenge led to rumours that New Order might appear, with Barney Sumner, Gillian Gilbert, Stephen Morris and Peter Hook all playing together in all three bands. Factory was quick to crush these rumours, but for a brief time, *Cities In The Park* seemed like the ultimate New Order dream concert.

Cities In The Park was held at Heaton Park in Manchester. Revenge performed 'Deadbeat' while Hook waved his arms to the music, but Electronic, according to reviews, put on a lacklustre show, despite the appearance of The Pet Shop Boys for 'Getting Away With It'. Happy Mondays stole the day where Electronic, or more properly New Order, should have. Factory bought the rights to release a live album of Sunday's concert, anticipating a street date in early 1992. Until then, the label whet appetites with *Martin*, a compilation of "The work of record producer Martin Hannett". Joy Division's 'She's Lost Control' and New Order's 'Everything's Gone Green' appeared on the disc, which came out on August 27.

The *Cities In The Park* LP idea was scrapped in favour of a videotape, and plans for a New Order reunion also fell through. Electronic released 'Feel Every Beat' on September 9, but the British compact discs were recalled due to a pressing error. Warner Brothers' American CD offered all of the assorted interpretations; a 'Single Remix', 'Tactile Mix', 'Downstairs Mix', 'UK 12" Remix', and 'DNA Remix'. Plus, it used two new B-sides, 'Lean To The Inside' (which sampled David Palmer's drums from ABC's 'Fear Of The World') and the deliriously good 'Second To None'. 'Feel Every Beat' was all right as an album track, and worked well in dance clubs, but as a single, it reflected diminishing returns. 'Getting Away With It', 'Get The Message', and now this. The news that Electronic were working with The Pet Shop Boys on a new track called 'Disappointed' seemed like a bit of a joke.

Busy recording 'Disappointed', Barney couldn't team up with New Order, so Peter Hook went in the studio with Revenge to write songs and rehearse for a tour. Stephen and Gillian threw up their hands in disgust. Besides doing soundtracks and appearing as spectators at events at the Hacienda, the duo had not been in the spotlight for over two years. Poking fun at Barney and Hooky's fame, they dubbed themselves the Other Two. The name spoke volumes about how they felt they were being viewed by their bandmates and the world.

The Other Two's début release, 'Tasty Fish', came out through Factory on October 28 and climbed up the Top Twenty independent singles chart. It was deservedly named a Single Of The Week by *New Musical Express*. Gillian's voice never sounded sweeter, having languished unused since the era of 'Procession' and 'Wheels Over Indian Trails'. The song itself, available on CD as a 'Pascal Mix', 'Pascal Mix 12', 'O.T. Mix 12', and 'Almond Slice Mix', placed a 'Round & Round'-ish melody atop a thumping dance beat. The chorus left everyone humming after just one listen: "No matter what you say, no matter what you do, it all comes back to you." The public liked this confection, but Tony Wilson didn't, telling Steve and Gillian, "We don't sell pop records." The Other Two felt ignored and unappreciated by Factory, which itself wasn't having the best of times.

New Order ✛ Joy Division

The label laid off five employees in October, 1991, and Wilson repeatedly denied reports that he was selling all or some of the label to London Records in order to cover company debts. The closure of the Hacienda and the effects of the recession on the record industry had drained Factory of money. *One True Passion* had sold poorly, never earning back all of the costs of recording the songs and filming 'Pineapple Face', and Factory only saw profits from British sales of *Electronic*. The label hoped albums by Happy Mondays and New Order would materialise to inject some well-needed capital.

Palatine, a four-disc, forty-nine-track box set retrospective of Factory's greatest hits and non-hits, seemed designed to fill in the void until then. Named after Palatine Road, the location of Factory's original offices, this big-ticket item ought to have revived the company's fortunes at least for a while. Sadly, the packaging proved difficult to manufacture, delaying *Palatine*'s release. Issued just in time to make it onto Christmas wish-lists – full-page ads began appearing in the first week of December – *Palatine*, subtitled, 'The Factory Story/1979-1990', did not even appear on the year-end album charts. Plundering the vaults did little to eradicate Factory's woes.

Revenge toured the UK as their new EP, the dumbly-titled *Gun World Porn*, was pushed back from a November to January release. Electronic played a one-off concert at Wembley Conference Hall 1. The Other Two worked on an album. Three years after 'Fine Time' redefined New Order, a year and a half after 'World In Motion' redefined them again, the band seemed no closer to playing together than they had been at the end of 1990.

Capitol Records released a 12" single of Revenge's 'State Of Shock' b/w 'Little Pig' to clubs on January 13, 1992, and to stores on January 22. As the promotional materials announced, "This studio recording utilises the expanded line-up to full effect, adding an even more aggressive edge to this guitar-driven dance band." Revenge was now composed of Peter Hook on bass and lead vocals, Chris Jones on keyboards, David "Pottsy" Potts on guitar and backup vocals, Mike Hedges on drums, and Brian Whittaker on supplementary bass guitar. The band had recorded the single as well as *Gun World Porn* in Hooky's basement, and the sound was rough and comfy. They got a nice vibe out of such primitive conditions.

The 12" began with the 'L'Pool Edit' and 'Paralized Mix' of 'State Of Shock', mixed by Keith Andrews at Liverpool's Amazon Studios. Bottom heavy and ambient, they were aimed squarely at club audiences. The 'EP Version', Revenge's original mix as intended for *Gun World Porn*, revealed the song as Hook, Jones, and Potts envisioned it: deceptively quiet at first, with imitation windchimes tinkling in the background, then rumbling with a full complement of basslines and drumbeats, pretty female vocals hovering angelically above the fray.

For the flipside, 'Little Pig', remix producer David Bianco fabricated an 'Extended Mix' by adding a jumble of nonsense tracks to the beginning and end of the song, and stretching out some instrumental sections. His intro was a nice touch, but he did not do much to improve the song – except to reveal Hook playing part of The Eagles' 'Hotel California' on his bass during the middle! 'Little Pig (EP Version)' clocked in at around two minutes less than the 'Extended Mix', and by cutting away the fluff, Hook's lyrics of unrequited love for another man's girlfriend were convincing. He sang, "I know that in time we'll kiss. It's the only thing you know is worth the risk." With that, he literally kissed the microphone, the sloppy, sucking noise bringing 'Little Pig' to a neat conclusion.

The 12" was nearly impossible to find in any store. Most copies that surfaced at second-hand shops were white-label promos sold by DJs who found the "aggressive edge" of Revenge too hard to take. The veiled, widow-like Revenge Girl on the sleeve almost served as a metaphor for the way this single died on the charts.

Gun World Porn did not do much better, and its failure was just as unwarranted. After 'Little Pig', an admittedly corny voice said, "I don't know about you, but I feel like dancing." This was the start of 'Cloud Nine', a song with a drumbeat sampled from George Harrison's cover version of 'Got My Mind Set On You' off his *Cloud Nine* LP – hence the title. 'State Of Shock' followed, then 'Deadbeat', the song Revenge had been performing on stage for much of the past year. This was more chaotic and violent than any track that had preceded it, Hook sticking by his beloved themes of shame and temptation. "The only way to end your life," he said, "is dive straight in and twist the knife." 'Deadbeat' ended as abruptly as it had begun, a weird whooshing noise sweeping from one speaker to the other.

A bonus track, Gary Clail's terrific remix of 'Deadbeat', removed much of the song's bluster but preserved and emphasised the vocal melody. The 'L'Pool Edit' and 'Paralized Mix' of 'State Of Shock', were revived, and *Gun World Porn* ended with an uncredited telephone answering machine message (similar to the one used at the start of 'Bleachman') which caught listeners off-guard. Strangely, the 'Extended Mix' of 'Little Pig' was not

included. If Capitol had hoped that making that song exclusive to the 12" would cause people to buy both releases in massive quantities, then their plan backfired miserably.

Revenge's new American press packet, which was sent to reviewers to generate publicity for the CD, included a newsletter, the *Gun World Porn Enquirer*, which transcribed interviews with Hooky and C.J. beneath headlines like "J.F.K. Visits Local K-Mart, Tells Shoppers He Has Returned For Revenge". C.J. defended his own contributions as well as Pottsy's, calling Revenge, "much more a democracy than the press would have you believe." Hooky's contribution, according to C.J. and the man himself, was as a sort of director who would, "check and channel", the ideas of his younger bandmates. The people in Revenge came across as honest-to-goodness friends, all grateful to play music with each other. One must imagine the early days of Joy Division were similarly heady.

Somebody should have checked and channelled Windsong Records' authorised LP of New Order's June 19, 1987 Glastonbury Fair concert where live footage had been shot for the video 'True Faith'. Generically titled *BBC Radio One Live In Concert*, this LP didn't sound much better than the *Hand Of God* double-album bootleg of the same gig which had

been circulating at record conventions for months. Windsong's single disc deleted the opening 'Elegia', plus magnificent renditions of 'Ceremony', 'Sub-Culture' and 'Sunrise', as well as much of New Order's between-song banter which had personalised this show. Most unforgivably, the album left out Peter Hook's vocal track! How could New Order, who had always maintained such high standards for their recordings, have permitted such a poorly-conceived work to be released? No answer was forthcoming from the band; they still had not reunited to work on a new LP, but were often gathered together in Factory's boardroom to discuss the health and future of the company.

A proposed LP by the Other Two was recorded but never put on sale, and the sole product of Electronic's labours since Autumn 1991 was 'Disappointed', a truly disappointing record on which Barney played keyboards but declined to sing. Neil Tennant performed the lead vocal, and the 'Single Mix', 'FBI Mix', and '808 Mix' all failed to click. Factory backed it with a remix of 'Idiot Country', while Capitol used an 'FBI Mix' of 'Gangster', which extended the album version to even grander proportions. The B-side offered substance where the A-side did not. 'Disappointed' also came out on the soundtrack of 'Cool World', the animated flop of the year. Neither the film nor the single lived up to expectations.

Into this bleak atmosphere of financial turmoil at Factory and poorly selling or poorly written or completely unreleased solo work, New Order met to do another LP. Factory's other big-name act, Happy Mondays, were recording at the same time, and both sessions required the label to invest huge amounts of cash without a like amount being recoupable for several months. No other act on Factory could sell enough records to match what New Order and the Mondays were spending on studio time, so it was up to those two bands to earn back their costs. After all previous sabbaticals, Gillian, Stephen, Barney and Hooky had been glad see each other. This time, the board meetings and rivalries between Revenge, Electronic and the Other Two reportedly stifled that joy. They all felt under pressure to bail Factory out of its financial troubles, like "battery hens" expected to lay eggs of gold. The urge to create music had been tainted by all of these external influences.

'A Factory Video', 'Here Are the Young Men' and 'Pumped Full Of Drugs', as well as other IKON titles, were re-released in the summer, perhaps as a last-ditch attempt to get cash. Now Tony Wilson really did have to meet with London Records and entertain their ideas about buying some or all of Factory, because a sale could help the label pay its creditors. Negotiations fell through when the discussion turned to New Order. Not unnaturally, London's interest in Factory was based primarily on the assumption that New Order would come as part and parcel of the deal. Representatives of London Records asked how much of a stake Factory owned in New Order. A document was produced, stating New Order completely and solely owned one hundred percent of their own music, and were free to leave at any time providing they gave Factory six months' notice. Without any assurance that New Order would stick with Factory if London Records bought the company, London broke communications with Factory and began dealing with New Order directly.

The band had fourteen musical ideas, ten electronic, four acoustic, by the time producer Stephen Hague was called in to help them develop and actually write the songs. New Order had written singles with Hague, John Robie, and Arthur Baker before, but had never relied on an outside source to co-write a complete LP. The band worked out of Stephen Morris' and Gillian Gilbert's home, Hooky coming over during the day and Barney the insomniac visiting at night to sing and play. Morris and Gilbert got very little sleep while accommodating their bandmates, and quickly grew tired of playing host and hostess. Hague strained everyone's nerves by asking the band to repeatedly go over their material until he could find the best performance. Any disagreements he had with the band about how to proceed with a track were won by a war of attrition: after innumerable takes, New Order gave up.

Happy Mondays' album ...Yes, Please came out months behind schedule, preceded by a mountain of bad publicity. Stories about crack addictions and the decline of acid house culture led to poor record and ticket sales for the band, and when the singles 'Stinkin' Thinkin'' and 'Sunshine And Love' went nowhere, Factory's £300,000 investment in the band's recording sessions looked unrecoverable. Only a New Order album could save the label, but the finished product – already assigned a Factory catalogue number, Fact 300 – had not yet been given to Wilson. New Order were negotiating with London Records to see if they could get a better deal with them than with Factory. The band neither wanted nor asked for the responsibility of saving Factory from bankruptcy. They waited for the inevitable.

On November 23, 1992, Factory Communications Limited went into receivership. Many creditors were left unpaid, and the receivers, Leonard Curtis, demanded that Factory's Charles Street office building go up for sale to help pay the label's £2,500,000 debt. Mancunian Tim Haves of Bernard Thorpe, the real estate firm entrusted to sell off the property, had the sad duty of hanging a For Sale sign outside the Factory windows. According to Haves, Tony Wilson and his employees did not go down weeping. "They had a massive party," Haves said. "They wrecked the whole boardroom table. It used to be suspended by wires; they just destroyed it. I got there one morning and it was a wreck. They left behind so much stuff: posters, records... they didn't need them and they left them." Only the Ben Kelly-designed boardroom chairs were spared.

Although Factory's headquarters were inappropriate for "normal" companies, Haves said there was considerable interest in making the building into a nightspot. "It was never going to go as an office. The people we had around it (wanting to buy the space) were all going to turn it into a club, using the Factory association. All of the breweries and architects looked at it. It was always going to be a club.

"The building sold for £430,000. Happy Mondays looked at it. They thought it would have been a stab at Tony Wilson for Happy Mondays if they bought it. The guy who manages the Happy Mondays was not a happy camper when I told him he couldn't have it cheap. He called me every name under the sun. He's obviously got a screw loose."

The people who bought the building were Peter Dalton and Carol Ainscrow, owners of the gay club Mantors. According to Haves, they converted it into the Paradise Factory, "a nightclub-cum-gallery, it's a bar... it's mainly going to be for homosexuals in Manchester."

In a strange act of karma, Happy Mondays broke up within weeks of Factory's closure, the victims of internal bickering. Other Factory bands remained homeless, including Vini Reilly, whose Durutti Column had been the whole reason for Tony Wilson and Alan Erasmus to start the Factory club in the first place. New Order made a deal with London Records, the details of which remained secret. It was simply announced that all future albums and singles would bear the inscription, "A New Order Release", and London was given the go-ahead to re-issue New Order and Joy Division's LP catalogue in the new year. The completed seventh album, the aborted Fact 300, was given an early 1993 shipping date.

New Order decided to release a single off the LP in April '93, first choosing 'The Price Of Love' (which they eventually re-titled 'World') and then opting for 'Regret'. 'Regret' was the stronger of the two, and was, in

Tony Wilson.

New Order ✛ Joy Division

New Order + Joy Division

fact, the best of the new songs they had recorded. It would all go downhill from here.

'Regret' began with a synthesizer and guitar playing an incredibly catchy riff off one another, each instrument completing the other's idea. Peter Hook's trademark bass and Stephen Morris' steady backbeat entered the conversation, topped by Barney's plea for a normal life after nearly two decades in the public eye and years of abusing his body. The final verse contained a thinly shrouded jab at Tony Wilson: "'Just wait 'til tomorrow'. I guess that's what they all say just before they fall apart." Finding heartbreaking beauty in the saddest of occasions, New Order once again proved themselves capable of writing the best pop songs on earth.

The single came out in a number of formats. 'The Album Version' was Hague's final mix, and it offered the most powerful, succinct rendition of all. 'The New Order Mix', although closer to the band's original concept, lacked Hague's single-mindedness and purity of vision. Four remixes also became available, 'The Fire Island Mix', 'Junior Dub Mix', 'Sabres Slow 'n' Low', and 'Sabres Fast 'n' Throb', all understated and mellow, befitting the current trend of ambient house music, which replaced acid house as the popular form. Hague's mix remained the best, charged as it was with vitality.

Video director Peter Care, known for his work with R.E.M., filmed the band in Rome, using visual symbols to illustrate the band's lyrics: a homeless person for "I would like a place I could call my own, have a conversation on the telephone"; newlyweds for " Wake up every day, that would be a start, I would not complain 'bout my wounded heart." New Order themselves were shot – miming – in an ornate Roman building. Barney eventually revolted against this pretension by giving the finger to the cameramen. Care, to his credit, left the scene in. It kept the video from taking itself too seriously.

The most startling thing about 'Regret' as a film was not that the bandmembers chose to lip-sync, but how old they all appeared. When photographed in 1991 as members of Electronic, Revenge and the Other Two, they all looked healthy and good for their age, all four of them being in their mid-thirties. In this video, and all photos taken in 1993, they seemed to have gained weight, Barney and Hooky had bags under their eyes, and none of them possessed the magnetism they'd had onstage in recent years. They all looked exhausted. Factory's collapse had debilitated them as much as Ian's death.

While in Italy to make the video, New Order began their most ambitious media campaign ever. The *NME*'s David Quantick attended the film shoots, and journalists from many countries spoke with the band at a press conference. One reporter from Austria asked, "Why did Ian Curtis kill himself?"

Hook, Gilbert, and Sumner were speechless. It was up to Stephen Morris to give the man a reply:

"He must have had a bad day, I suppose."

The publicity machine followed New Order home to England, where they spoke with entertainment magazines, and to California, where they cycled journalists and camera crews through their hotel rooms for a marathon session of short, one-on-one interviews. The band also performed 'Regret' on the beach set of *Baywatch* and sent it via satellite to *Top Of The Pops*. Repeatedly, the bandmembers were asked about their relationships with each other and the future of New Order. Would there ever be another new album after this one, already entitled *Republic*? They were not as close as they had been, the band admitted with disarming frankness. As far as releasing another album, they said they hoped to, but couldn't promise that they ever would. "What did Barney say?" became Hooky's new catchphrase. He had always been the bandmember most vocal about loving New Order, and he seemed genuinely worried about everyone else's morale, especially his best friend's.

The worst news to come from the interviews revealed that the band no longer enjoyed making music as much as they once had. The magic of creating songs had been their reason for existing, not fame or fortune. Without that need, New Order would die. The prospects for *Republic* were not too good.

Republic entered the UK charts at number one during the first part of May, 1993. 'Regret', already a Top Five hit, opened the disc with a bang. It stood out as a bit of an oddity, the only song on *Republic* to feature a "traditional" New Order combination of electronic and acoustic instruments. Peter Hook's bass would never reappear with such authority. Hague had the good sense not to tamper with the band's secret formula on 'Regret', but for the rest of the album, he would impose his own dance music ambitions on the songs, often at their expense.

On Malibu beach with
Baywatch star Daviud Hasslehoff.

In 'World', Barney sang, "I've no passion for this hate," and he seemed passionless for everything else as well. His voice dived deeper and reached higher than it ever had before, testament to his progress as a singer. Too bad the rest of the band weren't permitted the same liberties. Session musicans added background vocals, while synthesizers – and nothing else – provided the tunes. The basslines and guitar riffs, as well as the mistakes which had made New Order's earlier work so appealing were missing. Sonically if not spiritually, 'World' was sterile and antiseptic. 'Ruined In A Day' sampled drums and horns from Ennio Morricone's soundtrack to *The Good, The Bad, And The Ugly*, plus what sounds like the final note of 'Bizarre Love Triangle'. This cannibalism resulted in a bloodless dirge set to a disco backbeat. Only Barney evinced any life, his voice nearly exploding with anger. "Listen," he demanded, "I may be wrong but you'll listen." He proceeded to tell a morality tale of the hazards of being too free with one's inner feelings. Such honesty had apparently resulted in a betrayal in his life (by his wife Sue? Tony Wilson?). Wiser, or at least warier for the experience, the singer would now maintain absolute control over his life, keeping it in his own hands. What the acid house movement had set free in him, something occurring in the early 1990's had re-caged.

'Spooky' sounded suspiciously like Electronic, but Hook's bass appeared in tiny portions to remind listeners that this was New Order. The lyrics dealt with the importance of friendships, most likely those within the band, encouraging the audience to be fearless. In a similar vein, 'Everyone Everywhere' said, "At the end of the day there's no food on our plate," but that didn't matter as long as love remained. With a single kiss, a single breath, the problems of this world would be forgotten.

The lure to be part of a band or a family, and the need to exist alone, tugged Barney in opposite directions on 'Young Offender'. On one hand, he said, "Give me the freedom, I need to recover," and on the other, he swore, "Whatever it takes, I will make you mine." He sounded completely mixed up about how to proceed with his life. He also sounded like every other poor slob to fall for someone and be scared by the intensity of his own feelings.

New Order set their sights on Tony Wilson for 'Liar', bitching about the presence of MTV on Factory's television sets ("I can't stand the music always playing"), and hissing, "I haven't time to sympathise with all this nonsense and your lies." The band's venom for the man they dubbed 'King Of Nothing' was misplaced. Even if Wilson had been as inept or sneaky about running his company as this song would have one believe, what he may have lacked in business sense he made up for with a genuine, heartfelt enthusiasm for art. He always indulged New Order, Revenge, Electronic and Joy Division – his alleged treatment of the Other Two may have been thoughtless – and always spoke about Stephen Morris, Bernard Sumner, Gillian Gilbert, Peter Hook and Ian Curtis with pride, respect, and absolute trust in their character. Only New Order and Wilson himself knew what discussions occurred around the boardroom table during Factory's last days, but for the band to jab at him in this manner seemed undignified and distasteful. The music of 'Liar' was ingratiating, and New Order had every right to be angry at Wilson for not saving Factory, but the words they chose to express this anger reflected poorly on New Order as individuals.

'Chemical' pulsed with bass-heavy keyboard riffs. At first Barney accused, "Even though I give you special treatment, you keep getting high, juvenile delinquent," and then he made an overt reference to New Order: "It wasn't just the dream, it was much too good. Just another day in the brotherhood."

The all-conquering synthesizers stepped back during 'Times Change', allowing Hook's bass to creep through the mix, and the lyrics continued to hint at the fractures within New Order. But nothing could compare with the statements made during 'Special'. Here, Barney confessed, "It isn't what it used to be", "There's nothing left" and "I'm sick of trying, I mean that it's over." The chorus went right for the heart: "It was always special, it was like water down the drain." Could it be the band which now meant so little to them? For people whose lives had been changed by New Order's music, this concept was unbearable.

'Avalanche' put the album to rest without granting much hope for the future. A drone permeated the whole song, while tribalistic drums and a ceremonial keyboard phrase swept forward. Gillian intoned the word 'Faith', maybe encouraging fans to keep theirs. In the end, only the drone remained, similar to the one at the end of 'I Remember Nothing'. This time, there was no bottle or pipe thrown in anger. The noise just died, the plug pulled on New Order's most troubling album to date. *Movement* had been a disappointment, but the group had just been getting started when they recorded it. *Republic* was the result of New Order trying to force something out of themselves when they had nothing more to give. It was the awful sound of their friendship drying up.

Below: Bernard in Chicago, July 1993.

The shift from a "traditional" New Order sound which mixed dance music with rock to Hague's disco ideal took a while for many long-time fans to accept. Hooky's bass playing was sorely missed on most tracks, and while Barney's voice remained a band trademark, the instrumentation sounded quite anonymous. The songs on *Republic* were quite good, they just lacked the looseness and personality which had made earlier New Order material so wonderful. Had Hague conceded to the quartet's tastes rather than his own, *Republic* might have even rivalled *Technique*.

Peter Saville designed a booklet for the CD which presented contradictory images of life in that decaying fantasyland, California. Pristine mountain lakes blurred into rubble from the Los Angeles riots of 1992. A luxury car sped towards an inferno. A curl of saltwater with the phrase "Coming Up" printed over it looked like a tidal wave next to giant redwoods, tropical flowers, and a cityscape. The band especially liked the composite image on the cover: two young lovers yanking on a fluorescent life saver, nearly pulling it in half, while a home, maybe their own, went up in flames. These pictures reminded them of their own naïve power struggles within the band which seemed inconsequential compared to the disintegration of Factory.

Republic came out during early May, and in America, Qwest issued a special edition CD sub-titled *The Limited Run*. Only a few thousand copies were released. *The Limited Run* offered *Republic* as a full-colour picture disc CD housed in a spongy fluorescent orange package, reminiscent of the life saver on the LP sleeve. In a better economy, New Order fans might have snapped these artefacts up in a flash, but with wages in the US pretty much frozen or shrinking, not everyone could afford to lay out twenty-nine or thirty dollars for a really cool looking version of the same album they could buy for half the price in an ordinary plastic jewelbox. *The Limited Run* wasn't flying off the shelves much faster than *Gun World Porn*. *One True Passion*, meanwhile, had gone out of print because of lack of public interest, and tapes of *Electronic* could be found in bargain bins for a buck a copy. Tim Haves began letting out the offices above the Hacienda to outside sources because Factory still owed creditors lots of money. There were plenty of reasons for New Order to feel regret.

Out of respect for Barney's tour phobia, the band only scheduled thirteen concerts for 1993, one for each year of their existence. They began in early July, playing festivals in Germany, Dublin, Denmark and Montreux. Portions of the gigs were filmed for inclusion on a documentary of the quartet's history entitled *NewOrderStory*, which Paul Morley would write and produce. The band were also shot in Cannes by director Bailey Walsh, who they'd hired to make a video for 'World'. Then they hit North America for eight days at the Dallas Starplex, Shoreline Amphitheater, Hollywood Bowl, Chicago's World Music Theater, Toronto's Kingswood Music Theater, Washington, D.C.'s Merriwether Post, East Rutherford's Meadowlands Arena, and the Great Woods Performing Arts Center in Mansfield, Massachusetts. They were supported on various dates by 808 State and/or Sunscreem, plus guest appearances by Stereo MC's, The The, X, and The Judybats. The tour hit only a fraction of the cities with sizeable numbers of New Order fans, but the venues actually chosen were too big to be filled by the local fan populations. None of the gigs sold out.

Concurrent with the tour, London issued 'Ruined In A Day' as a single. It was available as two different CDs, sold separately but intended to go together as a set (the second volume came in a digi-pack with space to hold the first disc). Undoubtedly, this was the worst material New Order had ever put their names to. The remixes didn't even do justice to the original song, especially those by producers Sly and Robbie which dumped much of New Order's music and substituted an idiotic dance hall rap by another

artist. The non-LP track included on one CD, 'Vicious Circle (Mike Haas Mix)', seemed like an uncompleted demo but did not cast any light on New Order's creative process. A bunch of remixes which could have easily fitted onto one CD were being sold separately with little of New Order's influence evident on any cut. Fans were being asked to pay twice the amount they should have spent, and for substandard material.

Barney Sumner, Peter Hook, Stephen Morris and Gillian Gilbert left North America on August 6, 1993 for Manchester. 'World(The Price Of Love)' was released as a single on the 23rd. Like 'Ruined In A Day', the various remixes for this cut could have fit on a single CD, with room to spare, but instead were spread out over two discs. The 'Brothers In Rhythm Mix' extended the intro, allowing the mood to simmer for nearly two minutes before charging headlong into the pulsing body of the song. Hissing noises, a militaristic snare drum, siren-like synthesizers, and Barney's re-edited voice blended together, creating a sense of tension which amplified the impact of the fatalistic lyrics. The Brothers In Rhythm production team had crafted a smart new interpretation which preserved the song's intended message.

The 'Brothers Dubstramental' rearranged elements of this mix and dropped most of the vocals. The result was a novel bit of filler, but filler nonetheless. Likewise, the 'World In Action' and 'Pharmacy Dub' versions by K-Klass offered disco-friendly beats, but added nothing new to the song. Like so many remixes, emotional resonance had been sacrificed for the sake of making the track worthy for the dance floor. Steve Osbourne and Paul Oakenfold's 'Perfecto Mix', however, thrilled both the mind and hips by reinforcing New Order's original recording with additional vocal and instrumental tracks. The result: a high-tech sheen, a longer introduction and longer ending, all of which did not recraft the song as much as give the song's ideas a bigger forum. Osbourne and Oakenfold's 'Sexy Disco Dub' was a mostly instrumental reprise of the 'Perfecto Mix'. The 'Perfecto' and album versions were edited for radio airplay, bringing the available total number of non-LP mixes to eight.

Qwest issued half a dozen mixes – it neglected the 'Brothers Dubstramental' and 'Pharmacy Dub' – yet to get even just these six, fans had to purchase a CD maxi single and either a 12" or cassette maxi single, all of which overlapped some tracks. Two-track CD and cassette singles repeated songs found on their maxi-single counterparts. This begs the question: why did the band permit their record labels to spread out material over a variety of formats, when they could have saved their fans some money by placing everything onto one release? The price of love for American New Order fans who bought all five of Qwest's 'World' singles amounted to about $25.00. Had the band demanded that every mix be pressed on a single CD, those fans would have spent only six bucks.

The video for 'World' was filmed in crisp black and white within and around the Carlton Hotel on the French Riviera. New Order appeared in cameos. The camera panned by Peter Hook (seen beneath an umbrella), Barney Sumner (singing by a staircase), and Stephen Morris and Gillian Gilbert (both mugging for a photographer). The real stars were the elderly guests shown sunbathing and hiring prostitutes: paying a price for love. Without dialogue or even a central character through whom to tell the story, director Bailey Walsh conveyed a sense of loneliness. This suited the lyrics and mood of the song perfectly.

Hot on the heels of 'World' came New Order's final concert of 1994, held August 29 at the Reading festival. At the same time that the band were on stage, the documentary *NewOrderStory* was broadcast on TV – much to the chagrin of those fans attending the Reading gig! What concert goers missed was a cursory but enjoyable overview of the group's history, all linked together by rapturous narration written by Paul Morley. All four band-members spoke about their careers, as did Tony Wilson, Rob Gretton, Peter Saville, Neil Tennant, Quincy Jones, Arthur Baker, John Robie, U2 vocalist Bono, and others. The programme offered brief glimpses of archive footage of New Order and Joy Division, but not enough to satisfy and certainly far too little offstage material to offer glimpses into the musicians' personal lives. Inscrutable as ever, New Order stepped off the Reading stage as *NewOrderStory* came to an end, not to be seen together again in public for the rest of the year.

In the Fall of 1993, Peter Hook returned to Revenge, beginning work on their second full-length album. Barney Sumner disappeared from the public eye altogether. Stephen Morris and Gillian Gilbert, however, took centre-stage as The Other Two, promoting their new single 'Selfish' and forthcoming album *The Other Two & You* in the music press. 'Selfish'

turned out to be even better than the delightful 'Tasty Fish' thanks to Gillian's emotive voice and guitar playing, and Stephen's delicate, chiming keyboards. The melancholia they expressed in simple words and melodies distilled everything they'd learned about songwriting in New Order. The track would have fit easily on *Power, Corruption and Lies* or *Technique*. The remixes offered on the CD single highlighted Gillian's voice, making the squandering of her talents on *Republic* seem especially wasteful. Like Peter Hook, she'd emerged as a singer of equal ability to Barney Sumner, and she deserved to sing in the context of a New Order song just as much as anybody. The Other Two was the first project to give her voice the attention it deserved.

The American pressing of 'Selfish', released by Qwest, added a remix of the forthcoming album track 'Movin' On'. Bouncy and bass-heavy, it increased anticipation for the full-length LP. It wouldn't come out until 1994. At least fans could bide their time by watching the neat video made for 'Selfish'. It featured The Other Two in multiple roles: as boyfriend and girlfriend in a movie theatre, and as two actors in the film onscreen. Somebody in a gorilla suit starring in the "movie" pulled off his own mask to reveal a third Stephen Morris underneath, much to the embarrassment of the Stephen Morris watching in the theatre. MTV, clubs, and department stores all programmed the clip, and everyone who saw it loved the gentle goofiness of the piece.

The video made for New Order's 'Spooky' tried to be goofy too, but ended up being charmless. It was three minutes and 48 seconds of blue-tinted stop motion photography directed by Richard Heslop and produced by Kim Mnguni. New Order didn't appear; instead, 'Spooky' the video depicted quarrelling between the three clownish members of a love triangle. The audio track came from the 'Minimix' of 'Spooky' which opened the first disc of London's now-inevitable two-CD set. The 'Minimix' emphasised Barney's vocals, while the eerie 'Magimix' was built around numerous samples, and the 'Moulimix' sped up and slowed down for funny effect. None of these was essential to anyone but die-hard collectors. The second disc was the one to seek, if only for its 'Out Of Order' mix, which began dreamily with a melody which rose and fell, over and over, while a big bass drum thundered in the background. The implied feeling of doom was genuinely moving, and Barney's voice sounded very sad against this backdrop. The 'New Order In Heaven' mix stripped away the music at one point, leaving an *a capella* vocal. The 'Stadium Mix' and 'Stadium Instrumental' highlighted some of the backing tracks which had been overpowered by other instruments on the album version, and the 'Boo! Dub Mix' twisted song elements into a brand new composition. Qwest picked five of the mixes for its American release, adding an undistinguished 'Night Tripper Mix' for the 12" and an additional edit of the album version on the CD single. Once more, fans had to dig deep into wallets and purses to assemble a complete assortment of mixes. Perhaps the best thing to be said about the nearly three-dozen remixes created of *Republic*'s four singles is that they could help fans bide their time until the next New Order album, which the band hoped to record and release before the end of the century. After all, it might take a while to get bored with a song like 'Spooky' with eleven different versions to choose from.

The Other Two & You finally appeared in record shops on the first day of February, 1994. Although some of the tracks, like 'Tasty Fish', had been sitting around for over two years, every song glistened and sounded fresh. 'Tasty Fish' opened the collection, followed by a moody study of love and obsession called 'The Greatest Thing'. 'Selfish' came next, then the giddy 'Movin' On', which boasted terrific guitarwork by Andy Wroe and a magical falsetto by Gillian. 'Ninth Configuration', an instrumental first released on an October '93 sampler tape issued by *Lime Lizard* magazine, hearkened back to the duo's soundtrack work. At first spacious and ambient, it became busy and dynamic in a flash, then softened again and faded. At the drop of a pin, the Other Two could create pop songs or introspective new age soundscapes. Their ability to oscillate between these styles made *The Other Two & You* far more impressive than it would have been if it had only featured one or the other. The different textures they created complemented each other. The contrasts were fascinating.

'Feel This Love' opened with a throbbing, synthesized bassline. Gillian sang in the lower part of her vocal range, yearning for truth, new sensations, and the best life had to offer. All of these golden apples had tempted Ian Curtis, Barney Sumner, and Peter Hook in their songs. Gillian's quest was reflected in the creepy 'Spirit Level' and 'Night Voice' instrumentals, which sounded especially powerful when heard through headphones. Guitars howled, wisps of voices floated by like ghosts. 'Innocence' celebrated the conclusion of her rite of passage, leaving her, "Glad that it's all over" and re-energised. The album could have ended there, but the band chose to close with 'Loved It', subtitled 'The Other Track' to signify its incongruity with the rest of the album. This was a curious item which sounded like a sampled patchwork of New Order music and conversations. Somebody was plainly audible reciting part of 'World In Motion', and the speaking voices scattered throughout sounded like those of Barney Sumner, Gillian Gilbert, Peter Hook and Stephen Morris, with perhaps a bit of Rob Gretton thrown in for good measure. Whoever these mystery individuals were, they should have been proud to be part of such a brilliant album. *The Other Two & You* took Stephen and Gillian out of the shadows and declared them important voices in contemporary music. They would never be written off as "the other two" members of New Order ever again.

Whether or not they reunite and function as New Order or remain separated as members of their various solo projects, Barney Sumner, Peter Hook, Gillian Gilbert and Stephen Morris have shown every indication that they'll be making brilliant music into the twenty-first century. As the hearts of Electronic, Revenge, and The Other Two, they have written songs of remarkable beauty. As New Order, they have somehow combined their particular visions of what it means to live and die and fall in and out of love into something more wonderful than they could ever have produced on their own. Before they can again create New Order music, they need time to re-discover themselves, what they mean to each other and why they became friends in the first place. After all they've accomplished and all they've been through, there still must be some love that binds them together. When they remember that love, the songs will come easily. The dream is not over. They'll be back.

Selected Discography

The following is a subjective list of what I consider to be the best sampling of the recorded work of New Order, Joy Division, Electronic, Revenge, and The Other Two. I based my selections upon historical significance, rather than personal preference. They should give a general idea of the bands' roots and growth. Check your record store for domestic labels and catalogue numbers.

Joy Division: *Unknown Pleasures*
Disorder / Day Of the Lords / Candidate / Insight / New Dawn Fades / She's Lost Control / Shadowplay, Wilderness / Interzone / I Remember Nothing

Joy Division: *Closer*
Atrocity Exhibition / Isolation / Passover / Colony / A Means to an End / Heart and Soul / Twenty Four Hours / The Eternal / Decades

Joy Division: *Still*
Exercise One / Ice Age / The Sound Of Music / Glass / The Only Mistake / Walked In Line / The Kill / Something Must Break / Dead Souls / Sister Ray (live) / Ceremony (live) / Shadowplay (live) / A Means to an End (live) / Passover (live) / New Dawn Fades (live) / Twenty Four Hours (live) / Transmission (live) / Disorder (live) / Isolation (live) / Decades (live) / Digital (live)

New Order: *Movement*
Dreams Never End / Truth / Senses / Chosen Time / ICB / The Him / Doubts Even Here / Denial

New Order
Temptation b/w Hurt (Factory 7-inch vinyl single / out of print)

New Order: *Power Corruption and Lies*
Age Of Consent / We All Stand / The Village / 5.8.6. / Your Silent Face / Ultraviolence / Ecstasy / Leave Me Alone

New Order: *Low-Life*
Love Vigilantes / The Perfect Kiss / This Time Of Night / Sunrise / Elegia / Sooner Than You Think / Sub-Culture / Face Up

New Order: *Brotherhood*
Paradise / Weirdo / As It Is When It Was / Broken Promise / Way Of Life / Bizarre Love Triangle / All Day Long / Angel Dust / Every Little Counts

New Order: *Substance*
Ceremony / Everything's Gone Green / Temptation (new version) / Blue Monday / Confusion (new version) / Thieves Like Us / The Perfect Kiss / Sub-Culture (remix) / Shellshock / State of the Nation / Bizarre Love Triangle (extended version) / True Faith / In a Lonely Place / Procession / Mesh / Hurt / The Beach / Confusion (instrumental) / The Kiss Of Death / Shame Of the Nation / 1963

Salvation! Original Motion Picture Soundtrack
New Order contribute: Salvation Theme / Touched By the
Hand Of God / Let's Go / Sputnik / Skullcrusher

Joy Division: *Substance*
Warsaw / Leaders Of Men / Digital / Autosuggestion /
Transmission / She's Lost Control (version) / Incubation / Dead
Souls / Atmosphere / Love Will Tear Us Apart / No Love Lost /
Failures / Glass / From Safety to Where / Novelty / Komakino /
These Days

New Order
Blue Monday 1988 b/w Touched By the Hand Of God

New Order: *Technique*
Fine Time / All the Way / Love Less / Round & Round / Guilty
Partner / Run / Mr. Disco / Vanishing Point / Dream Attack

Joy Division: *The Peel Sessions*
Exercise One / Insight / She's Lost Control / Transmission / Love
Will Tear Us Apart / Twenty Four Hours / Colony / Sound Of Music

New Order: *The Peel Sessions*
Truth / Senses / I.C.B. / Dreams Never End / Turn the Heater On /
We All Stand / Too Late / 5.8.6.

New Order
World In Motion / World In Motion (The B-side)

Revenge: *One True Passion*
Pineapple Face / Big Bang / Kiss the Chrome / Slave / Bleachman /
Surf Nazi / 7 Reasons / Fag Hag / It's Quiet

Electronic: *Electronic*
Idiot Country / Reality / Tighten Up / The Patience Of a Saint /
Getting Away With It / Gangster / Soviet / Get the Message / Try All
You Want / Some Distant Memory / Feel Every Beat

Revenge: *Gun World Porn*
Little Pig / Cloud Nine / State Of Shock / Deadbeat / Deadbeat
(Gary Clail Remix) / State Of Shock (L'Pool Edit) / State Of Shock
(Paralized Mix)

New Order
Regret / World / Ruined In a Day / Spooky / Everyone
Everywhere / Young Offender / Liar / Chemical / Times Change /
Special / Avalanche

The Other Two: *The Other Two & You*
Tasty Fish / The Greatest Thing / Selfish / Movin' On / Ninth
Configuration / Feel This Love / Spirit Level / Night Voice / Loved It
(The Other Track)

New Order: *The Best Of New Order*
True Faith 1994 / Bizarre Love Triangle 1994 /　　　 /
Regret / Fine Time / The Perfect Kiss / Shellsh　　 ves
Like Us / Vanishing Point / Run 2 / Round & Ro　　　 World /
Ruined In A Day / Touched By The Hand Of Go　　 onday
1988 / World In Motion

Selected Videography

The following home videos offer the best selection of film
footage of New Order and Joy Division commercially available.
Several compilations featuring one or two songs have been
left out, because the titles listed below do an equal or better
job of capturing the groups' performances.

Joy Division: *Here Are The Young Men*
From Safety to Where? / Decades / Dead Souls (live) /
Love Will Tear Us Apart (live) / Shadowplay (live) / Day Of
the Lords (live) / Digital (live) / Colony (live) / New Dawn Fades
(live) / Autosuggestion (live) / Transmission (live) / Sound Of Music
(live) / She's Lost Control (live) / They Walked In Line (live) /
I Remember Nothing (live) / Love Will Tear Us Apart

New Order: *Taras Shevchenko*
ICB (live) / Dreams Never End (live) / Everything's Gone Green
(live) / Truth (live) / Senses (live) / Procession (live) / Ceremony
(live) / Little Dead (live) / Temptation (live) / Confusion

New Order: *Pumped Full Of Drugs*
Confusion (live) / Love Vigilantes (live) / We All Stand (live) /
As It Is When It Was (live) / Sub-Culture (live) / Face-Up (live) /
Sunrise (live) / This Time Of Night (live) / Blue Monday (live)

New Order: *Substance*
The Happy One / Confusion / The Perfect Kiss / Shellshock /
Bizarre Love Triangle / True Faith / Touched By the Hand Of God /
Blue Monday 1988

New Order: *Academy*
(recalled because art had not been approved)
Bizarre Love Triangle (live) / The Perfect Kiss (live) / Ceremony
(live) / Dreams Never End (live) / Love Vigilantes (live) / Confusion
(live) / Age Of Consent (live) / Temptation (live) / Temptation (reprise)

New Order: *NewOrderStory*
Fine Time / Round & Round / Run / World In Motion / Regret /
World / Atmosphere / Transmission (live) / Love Will Tear Us Apart /
Ceremony (live) / Temptation (live) / Blue Monday (live) / Blue
Monday (Sunkist commercial) / Shellshock / Age Of Consent /
State Of the Nation / True Faith / Ruined In A Day / Atmosphere

Interviews

I am especially indebted to the following individuals who took
the time to share with me their memories and thoughts about
New Order and Joy Division: Peter Saville (September 30,
1986, White Columns, Manhattan), Robert Gretton (November 5,
1988, Sunset Marquis Hotel, Los Angeles), Michael Shamberg
(November 20, 1988, Cascondo Studios, Manhattan), Tony Wilson
(November 25, 1988, Sunset Marquis Hotel, Los Angeles), Tom
Atencio (January 20, 1989, Los Angeles), Tim Haves (July 30,
1993, Bernard Thorpe, Manchester).

Selected Bibliography

Although I used literally hundreds of articles, reviews,
advertisements and documents during the writing of this
biography, many items came from private collectors and individuals
close to the band, and could not all be traced back to their
original sources. Rather than include an incomplete listing of
magazine and newspaper articles, *et. al*, I have limited my
bibliography to the interviews I conducted and some of the books
to which I referred.
Information from pretty much every news item I could find relating
to New Order, Joy Division, Electronic, Revenge and the Other
Two from the past ten years was written into a timeline, considered for importance and validity, and either used to tell the bands'
history or was discarded as irrelevant. Whenever possible, I tried
to get recollections and insights from persons with first-hand
knowledge of what happened.

Books

I can't recommend enough that fans of New Order and Joy
Division investigate these titles, all of which proved valuable in
researching information for *Dreams Never End*:

Broll, Marco, *Joy Division*, Stampa Alternativa, Rome (no date
given). Edge, Brian, *Pleasures and Wayward Distractions*,
Omnibus Press, London, 1984; and, in an updated edition, 1988.
Johnson, Mark, *An Ideal For Living*, Proteus Books, London,
1984; subsequently republished by Bobcat Books, 1988.Suatoni,
Alfredo, *From the Centre Of the City*, Stampa Alternativa, Rome,
1989. West, Mike, *Joy Division*, Babylon Books, Lancashire, 1984.